Contents

Rights, needs and the user perspective

A review of the National Health Service and Community Care Act

Edited by Sue Balloch, Jabeer Butt, Mike Fisher and Vivien Lindow

National Institute for Social Work and the Joseph Rowntree Foundation

Rights, needs and the user perspective:
A review of the National Health Service and
Community Care Act 1990

Published 1999
by the National Institute for Social Work
5 Tavistock Place, London WC1H 9SN
www.nisw.org.uk
email info@nisw.org.uk

The Joseph Rowntree Foundation has supported this
project as part of its programme of research and
innovative development projects, which it hopes will
be of value to policy makers and practitioners. The
facts presented and views expressed in this report,
however, are those of the authors and not necessarily
those of the Foundation.

ISBN 1 899942 33 5

Cover designed by Pat Kahn

Printed by Meridian Print Centre Ltd, Derby

Acknowledgements

The Editors of this review of the NHS and Community Care Act 1990 are grateful to the Joseph Rowntree Foundation for the funding which made it possible. They could not, however, have carried out the review without the support and contributions of those who are acknowledged below. Through their comments on the first draft of the review, discussion of the key issues which arose from these in a seminar on 19th January 1999, and written contributions, these individuals ensured that a diversity of perspectives were reflected. Some of these are included in boxed quotes in various sections of the text. Our special thanks are due to those service users who emphasised the importance of users' knowledge of community care and used their expertise to assess the progress made and difficulties arising since 1993. We also express our gratitude to NISW staff: to Daphne Statham for chairing the seminar; to those who organised and took notes during the seminar – Rachael Frank, Martin Heidensohn and Fung-yee Lee; to Rose Freeman who carried out all the secretarial tasks involved in preparing the final review; to Library and Information Service staff Sue Jardine and Angela Upton who helped with the literature; and to Margaret Hogan for proof reading this text and arranging its publication.

Contributors to the review

Jane Belman
London Voluntary Service Council

Peter Beresford
Open Services Project

Peter Blackman
National Development Officer, SIA

Ian Bradford
Care & Repair England

Don Brand
National Institute for Social Work

Phil Brough
Shropshire Disability Forum

Doreen Crockford
Salvation Army

Clare Evans
Disabled People's Forum, Leonard Cheshire

Steve Griffiths
Independent Consultant

Fiona Hackland
Standing Conference on Drug Abuse

Tessa Harding
Help the Aged

Frances Hasler
National Centre for Independent Living

Enid Levin
National Institute for Social Work

John McCracken
Department of Health

Jo Moriarty
National Institute for Social Work

Mary Nettle
Independent Consultant

Dr Chai Patel
Governor, NISW

M.T. Phung
Islington Social Services Department

Gwen Rosen
National Institute for Social Work

Angela Sinclair
Islington Older People's Forum

Daphne Statham
National Institute for Social Work

Jenny Stiles
Relatives Association

Michael Turner
Shaping Our Lives, NISW

Ayesha Vernon
Social Policy Research Unit, University of York

Peter Williams
Shaping Our Lives, NISW

The Editors

Sue Balloch
University of Brighton

Jabeer Butt
Race Equality Unit

Mike Fisher
National Institute for Social Work

Vivien Lindow
Independent Consultant

Chapter 1

Introduction

The official history

Following the Griffiths Report (DoH, 1988) the basic principle for the provision of community care was set out in 1989 in the Government's White Paper *Caring for People* which stated that anyone needing health or social care because of problems associated with old age, mental illness, or learning, physical or sensory disabilities, should be able to obtain care and support tailored to their individual needs. This should then enable them to live in their own home with as much independence as possible or in residential accommodation. High quality public services were to be promoted within an economy of mixed provision. Better support was also to be provided to carers.

The National Health Service and Community Care Act 1990 which came into force on 1st April 1993 provided the framework for the assessment of care needs and the arrangement of services by local authority social services departments. Duties placed on local authorities through the Act included:

- to produce and publish a community care plan and consult with other agencies;

- to assess individual need for the community care services covered by the Act and, following assessment, consider the provision of services to match individual needs;

- to inspect premises used for community care services;

- to establish a complaints procedure.

Policy guidelines set out by the Act provided for:

- support for the user in his/her own home including day and domiciliary care, respite care, the provision of disability equipment and adaptations to accommodation as necessary;

- a move to more suitable accommodation, which might be sheltered or very sheltered housing, with social services support;

- a move to another private household, with relatives or friends or as part of an adult fostering scheme;

- residential home care;

- nursing home care;

- long stay care in hospital.

The Act does not stand alone as a piece of legislation and must be considered along with numerous other acts, regulations, directions and guidance issued by the Secretary of State. These include:

- The National Assistance Act 1948, Part III, Section 21

- The Health Services and Public Health Act 1968

- The Chronically Sick and Disabled Persons (CDSP) Act 1970 and the Disabled Persons (Services, Consultation and Representation) Act 1986

- The National Health Service Act 1977

- The Mental Health Act 1983

- The Health and Social Services and Social Security Adjudications Act 1983

- The Carers (Recognition and Services) Act 1995

- The Community Care (Direct Payments) Act 1996.

The Act also needs to be considered along with changes in social security legislation, as it was driven in part by growing concern over the huge increase in social security expenditure on residential and nursing home fees that followed the Residential Homes Act 1984. As Fran Bennett has put it, 'In this view, the decision of the Government to grant the lead role in community care to local authorities did not so much represent a devolution of power and control from central to local government, as a divestment of a particularly problematic policy area' (Bennett, 1996 p.15).

Rights, needs and the user perspective

Recognising that there are many groups with a stake in the new arrangements introduced by the 1990 Act, we have tried in this review to reflect the diverse and sometimes contradictory perspectives and experiences of a wide range of stakeholders and record what they think has really been taking place.

The thinking behind this legislation can be characterised as seeking a better implementation of existing models of service provision, rather than questioning the very basis for community care services. In this sense the 1990 Act implemented the critiques of the 1980s and in no way laid the foundations for any of the new approaches that have gained authority in the 1990s and which contributors have illustrated throughout this review.

Foremost among these has been the growth of service user groups, particularly among disabled people, and their development of a social, as opposed to a medical, model of disability. Along with this, one of the most urgent and clear messages from the service user constituency to emerge from the consultations underpinning this review is the need to explore the rights-based, instead of the needs-based, model of community care.

The rights-based model of community care links directly with the concept of citizenship, re-emergent as the basis of entitlement to services in response to the sustained attack on social welfare that began in the 1980s.

Citizenship demands that people may expect support and care from society primarily because of their membership of it and contribution to it, not because of their needs. This thinking has underpinned the development of the user movement in modern social welfare policy and is particularly well demonstrated by direct payments.

The right to welfare as a citizen brings with it other rights, such as the right to evaluate how assessments should be undertaken and by whom, how eligibility criteria should be set, and for what purposes services should be developed. It brings the clear expectation that the receipt of community care services will not diminish entitlement to the kind of life and opportunities that all members of society wish to enjoy.

Rights and needs do not operate independently and thus cannot be treated as totally exclusive issues. Our rights to services will not be exercised unless we are in need, and exercising our rights may put us in competition with others in any situation where resources are finite. Much of the discussion turns on funding, and it is the underfunding of many community care services that this review demonstrates. The debate over providing preventative services for large numbers of people, as opposed to targeting services on those fewer numbers in greatest need, is about how to spend limited resources most effectively, regardless of rights.

This was well illustrated in the Judicial Review of Gloucester County Council's decision to tighten its eligibility criteria for domiciliary services in order to stay within its budget. As a consequence the County withdrew services from those previously assessed as being in need of services and who had been receiving them. The decision was condemned and contested by service users but has been upheld by the present Government.

Citizens do not live in isolation, and rights and needs have therefore to be considered in terms of families and communities, and the mutually responsible and caring relationships which individuals develop. There was little thought in the framing of the community care legislation to foster the responsibilities of communities to create services for citizens. Modern thinking about care emphasises the concept of interdependence, or mutuality, rather than portraying some people as dependent on the care of others. This recognises both the lifetime likelihood that all of us will experience the need for care at some time in our adult lives, and that giving care should be seen essentially as an exchange, even where that exchange is starkly unequal. This means that there should be as much discussion of the ways in which community regeneration and mutuality can provide an environment in which people can have their needs met, as there is of the ways of helping people to care for others.

Because of this perspective, this review has not focused on the needs of carers. The recently launched National Strategy for Carers has done this very successfully and represents over a decade of lobbying by carers associations. Many service users have, however, been angered by the importance accorded to carers, perceiving this as being over and above their own needs. The Carers Strategy, for example, speaks strongly about meeting carers' needs for respite and does not acknowledge that a user's needs for respite from a carer may be just as great. We see this as one of the major unresolved tensions in the community care debate.

The changing agenda

Since the Labour Government came to power in May 1997 there have been changes in the policy agenda. A constant stream of documents has emphasised that health, housing and social services must work in closer partnership, observe the principles of Best Value and encourage the involvement and participation of service users. Among more recent publications, the White Paper *Modernising Social Services* and the Report of the Royal Commission on Long Term Care (1999) have stimulated the debate on the funding and delivery of community care services. Although some of their proposals are radical, both documents reveal that the Government remains committed to the mixed economy of care and to means testing older people for services other than health . This is in contrast to the Royal Commission's majority recommendation that all should also have a right to free personal care after assessment throughout their lives. It is clear that we currently lack a consensus about the role of the state in creating and sustaining community care services, which in turn makes it vital that the continuing debate takes full account of the diverse views of a wide range of stakeholders.

About the review

In this review our focus has been on England and Wales, the countries to which this legislation applied. We began with a selective literature review carried out by staff of the Library and Information Service at the National Institute for Social Work (NISW). Our approach was then to engage in dialogue with key stakeholders from user, carer and black communities. The editorial group, which included two co-authors from user and black communities, prepared a short discussion paper to distribute to a wide range of stakeholders for comment. This original paper covered a brief summary of the purposes of the legislation and subsequent amendments, changes in the roles of statutory, voluntary and private agencies, success stories and the growth of concern among users, carers, black communities and the general public about issues ranging from funding and charging for services to the interface between social services, health and housing. Specific sections were contributed by the co-editors and colleagues.

We invited up to thirty readers of this paper from user groups and the National User Group, members of the National Community Care Alliance, officers and governors of the National Institute for Social Work, representatives of private care organisations, directors of social services, the Department of Health and relevant researchers. Readers, authors and editors then met for a seminar on 19th January 1999 to discuss the paper and the extensive written comments which had been circulated. The seminar identified omissions and issues to be expanded in the original paper, drew in further contributions, notably on older people, housing, drugs and substance misuse, and strengthened the emphasis on users' rights. The boxed inserts in Chapters 2 and 4 are comments made by the contributors to the seminar. Thus the views of service users, service providers and local policy makers infuse the review. The only view significantly under represented is of central policy makers, and that is because we wanted to question the public policy statements on the implementation of the legislation, particularly those made to the Royal Commission on Long Term Care.

We commence the review with an analysis by Mike Fisher of some of the key issues which have dominated the implementation of community care in this decade (Chapter 2). This is followed by Sue Balloch's discussion of identifying need (Chapter 3). Vivien Lindow penetrates to the heart of the review with a critique of the continuing failure of community care to involve service users equally and effectively (Chapter 4). Jabeer Butt builds a picture of the developments that have taken place since 1990 in community care services for black communities (Chapter 5). Jo Moriarty assesses developments in community care that have both benefited and disadvantaged older people (Chapter 6) and continues her discussion with a focus on older people with dementia and their carers (Chapter 7). Don Brand looks at community care policy and practice for people with learning difficulties (Chapter 8). Sue Balloch probes issues around rationing and charging (Chapter 9). Ian Bradford and Sue Balloch examine the changing role of housing in community care (Chapter 10). Fiona Hackland illustrates the problems integral to community care and substance misuse service provision (Chapter 11). Enid Levin concentrates on the impact of the Act from the perspective of social services departments and their staff (Chapter 12). Finally, in the conclusions, the editors draw out the major themes to emerge from the review and implications for the future (Chapter 13).

This section draws on the following sources:

Bennett, F. (1996) *Highly Charged: Policy issues surrounding charging for non-residential care,* York: Joseph Rowntree Foundation.

Coote, A. (1992) *The Welfare of Citizens*, London: Rivers Oram Press.

Department of Health (1998) *Community Care: An agenda for action* (The Griffiths Report), London: HMSO.

Royal Commission for Long Term Care (1999) *With Respect to Old Age: Long term care – rights and responsibilities*, Cm.4192, London: The Stationery Office.

Secretary of State (1989) *Caring for People,* London: HMSO.

Secretary of State (1998) *Modernising Social Services: Promoting independence; improving protection; raising standards,* Cm.4169, London: The Stationery Office.

Chapter 2

Some key issues

Mike Fisher

The influence of the NHS and Community Care Act 1990

In many respects, it is not the Act itself which is the major influence on the arrangements for community care. Most of the Act is concerned with establishing health care trusts and the financial arrangements for the 'new' NHS. Of 67 sections, only nine address community care in England and eight community care in Scotland. However, the Act spawned a host of guidance documents, which were extremely influential in defining the parameters, for example, of care management and the purchaser/provider relationship. A legitimate question is whether this array of guidance was subject to the same safeguards of democratic debate as the Act itself, and whether it accurately reflects the interests of different stakeholders.

Subsequent legislation concerning the right to assessment among some carers, the Disability Discrimination Act, and direct payments have probably had a much greater effect on community care arrangements, and may reflect much more strongly the interests of particular groups (even if the legislation does not always match their expectations). The proposed 'reforms' to the Mental Health Act 1983, particularly the introduction of compulsion in the community, will also impact on the lives of people with mental health problems far beyond anything in the NHS and Community Care Act. The investment and principles underlying the sections of the White Paper on *Modernising Social Services* covering services to adults will have similarly far-reaching impact.

In parallel, the practical interpretation within social services departments of their responsibilities, and the pressures on the health service leading to its withdrawal from long term care and to early discharge policies, have probably done more to shape community care than any legislation or guidance. Even if we attempt to read legislative intent, the shape of community care is more strongly determined by subsequent policy and practice than by the sections of the Act. It would be a mistake, therefore, to see this review as narrowly concerned with the text of the Act, or primarily with the principles its architects hoped it would enshrine.

Choice, autonomy and reform

Enhancing choice was an explicit goal of the new arrangements for community care. Needs-led assessment would lead to packages of care 'in line with individual needs and preferences', and increased use of private and voluntary providers would 'widen consumer choice'. We will assess later whether this has materialised, but what is often forgotten is that the new arrangements were designed partly to restrict independent choice – that is, to prevent people from choosing which residential care provider they would use at public expense without having to be assessed by a social services worker. Had older people in particular been asked whether they wished to trade their existing choice for the safeguard of a social services assessment, it is far from clear that they would have chosen the latter.

The current review of the mental health legislation will lead to a substantial reduction of autonomy if proposals for community-based compulsion (deemed 'non-negotiable' by the Minister) are implemented. These include legalising treatment by psychiatrists without the citizen's consent outside hospital and giving powers to assist with the enforcement of this treatment. In parallel, there is a burgeoning interest in the criminal aspects of psychiatry. For people with mental health problems, the current direction is unmistakably towards greater coercion, not towards greater choice.

Ambivalence towards the public sector

The new arrangements for community care were carried through by an administration deeply suspicious of the role of public officials in providing welfare. The influential 'new public management' suggested that public services needed an infusion of business principles: trust, teamwork and professional ethics were to be replaced by contracts, performance indicators and bonuses. Quite apart from the serious question whether there was any evidence to support this theory, what was remarkable was its power to undermine the motivation of the very people providing services who were to be asked to change their fundamental working practices. If sound business practice was to be the watchword, we might have expected some serious attention to the single most valuable asset in a restructured personal social services – the motivation and commitment of the workforce.

Similarly, we might have expected some serious analysis of the skills and knowledge required at different levels of the service. Instead, the reforms were underpinned by the claim that 'there may in fact be a tendency to over elaborate, both as to the professional input and the training required. Many of the needs of elderly and disabled people are for help of a practical nature (getting dressed, shopping, cleaning)'. Little attention was given to the question of an appropriately educated and trained workforce or to the analysis of the levels of skills and knowledge required for community care. Only recently has detailed information about the working experiences of the social services workforce, for example, become available, from the NISW Workforce Studies (Balloch, McLean and Fisher, 1999), and recognition been offered that social care requires a human resources strategy.

A flourishing independent sector

The concept of the mixed economy as a new development, or of informal sources as the new mainstay of care provision, struck a discordant note in many quarters. For black and minority ethnic group communities, non-statutory care had become the only source of appropriate care, given the inability or unwillingness of statutory providers to change underlying ethnocentric assumptions. There was anger amongst these communities that this was not recognised, and that the White Paper did not propose specific measures to direct funding to support these sources of care. Jabeer Butt expands on this in his overview of the experiences of black and minority ethnic group communities (Chapter 5).

A similar argument applies to older people. Since the 1960s, study after study has shown that the primary source of care for older people is other older people, usually a spouse. If not by an older person, care is most likely to be provided by a female member of kin. In this context, the concept of informal care does not represent new thinking, but rather a recognition of the status quo. Older people and their carers might have expected more resources in support of this principle, rather than a statement of what, to them, must have been obvious.

Laing and Buisson's analysis prepared for the Royal Commission on Long Term Care suggests that the trend is towards larger providers in home care, and that the demand for residential care will drop in the near future before rising again, leading to a consolidation of suppliers in this sector. The proposed conditions for a successful independent sector make chilling reading: they include major cost savings by independent providers in the lower wages to care workers (notwithstanding the effects of the national minimum wage), and the injunction to social services departments to set a price level that will ensure providers an adequate return on investment. It seems this sector of the market cannot flourish without low wages and a degree of protection by the public sector.

The changing role of the voluntary sector

There have also been concerns about the changing role of the voluntary sector. Although the new arrangements for community care envisaged an expanding role for the voluntary sector, this was to be closely managed by social services departments. In addition, it was intended that there should be greater diversity of voluntary sector providers in order to address the needs of a wide range of service users. These two factors have had some far-reaching consequences for the sector.

First, the 'contract culture' has led to close supervision of voluntary sector provision, and correspondingly detailed accountability processes. Greater attention may sometimes be paid to reporting and contract observance than to the spirit of what was intended to be the provision. In turn, energy that was once directed towards innovation often has now to be directed towards monitoring and preparing for the next proposal for funding. A traditional role of the voluntary sector in undertaking risky services and in experimenting with untried approaches has become less feasible. The voluntary sector providers themselves are concerned that they may increasingly be used to meet statutory obligations at minimal cost.

Secondly, the diversity of providers brings the possibility that funding will be distributed in smaller chunks to more agencies. This may mean that pilot services are initiated without clear long term commitment to maintain services to groups that have been newly reached. It may also mean an increased dependency on the social services funding cycle, and turn voluntary providers' attention more towards satisfying their funders than towards building community commitment in support of marginalised groups.

Thirdly, some providers may not be sufficiently exposed to some of the movements reshaping mainstream service provision. For example, some may have little experience of including service users as fully empowered participants on their management committees. In the context of pressure from commissioners to provide value for money, these providers may also have little incentive to engage in this kind of structural reform that may increase costs in the short term.

Lastly, the focus on social services funding leaves less time, energy and opportunity to address policy at the national level. New developments in social welfare may thus be less subject to the traditional scrutiny and reality-testing that voluntary sector pressure groups have brought to policy development.

The purchaser/provider split

The distrust of the public sector's role in welfare underpinned the implementation of the purchaser/provider split. The thinking was that purchasers must not be providers because they would favour the existing services which they themselves provide, thus preventing either (a) value for money, or (b) diversification of providers, particularly in the private and voluntary sectors. Although there is no requirement in the legislation to effect a purchaser/provider split, Department of Health guidance required social services to implement 'the objectives of separation'. A small survey by the Local Government Information Unit (LGIU, 1997) of home care showed that most departments felt that they should implement this split either to remain at the forefront of management development in community care, or in order to avoid being obliged to implement it later in ways in which they would not have chosen. Half of the departments surveyed by LGIU had implemented what they called a 'pure' split, involving a complete divorce of the two roles of providing and assessing, while the other half had hybrid systems. In both there were substantial problems of duplication, of the loss of expertise of front line assessors, and problematic relations between providers and assessors. Similar evidence is available from the study by Lewis and Glennerster (1996), where departments were shown to operate a variety of mechanisms directed more at the appearance of a separation of functions.

The LGIU study of home care also reported improved consistency in assessment, a wider range of services, and improved financial management. However, in the absence of effective evaluation, it is impossible to know whether these benefits derive directly from the implementation of a split or from some other source. Given the emphasis on high quality assessment, and given the fact that the purchaser/provider split often removes from the assessment process the most highly skilled front line workers, it is difficult to perceive a continuing rationale for this structural separation of assessing for services and providing them. In particular, it is necessary to examine how the continuing involvement of the practitioner undertaking the assessment in the subsequent provision of services might improve the original assessment and/or improve the benefit which the service user derives from the service.

The creation of older people as 'the problem'

The implementation of the NHS and Community Care Act 1990 has coincided with a theme in official policy that the state can no longer afford to support older people. The concept of the 'rising tide' of older people and the portrayal of expenditure on this group as an impossible burden on those in work lay behind the Conservative Government's decision to drop the link between earnings and state pensions in 1980, and behind the 1996 decision by the Labour opposition to remove the restoration of the link from its manifesto. As many commentators have pointed out, the so-called 'dependency' ratio has not changed substantially since 1900, and the probable period when there will be a substantial increase in over 85s is 2025-30. The Royal Commission on Long Term Care (1999) suggests that 'for the UK there is no 'demographic timebomb' ... and as a result of this the costs of care will be affordable'. Ermisch commented three years before the implementation of the community care legislation that 'it appears that standards of service could be maintained with only a 12% increase in resources over a period of 40 years. This is a trivial increase in expenditure compared with the 14% increase in real expenditure on these services [health and personal social services] during 1980-88' (Ermisch, 1990 p.10). Thus there is a substantial planing period, several options and no need for immediate cutbacks.

It is in any case inappropriate to regard older people as a drain on resources, when, as has been suggested above, they constitute the major source of care to older people. Older people also provide a very significant resource to the younger generation, in both cash and kind. Furthermore, it is perverse to develop health and welfare services and then to complain that those most in need — older people — use them. Jack (1991) demonstrates the ageism inherent in such a view by identifying the lack of public outcry over the predominant use of the education system by young people. The consequence is that we should not accept without critical analysis that a key role of the new arrangements for community care is to reduce public expenditure on older people, nor that effective targeting of scarce resources should mean the barring of access to services to all except those in dire need. Any review of the implementation of community care should constantly question the assumption that we cannot afford to provide appropriate services to the largest user group — older people. If we have the political will, we have the resources and the time to secure better services.

Targeting and prevention

It is generally suggested that one of the successes of the new arrangements for community care has been greater efficiency in targeting scarce resources on those most in need. For example, the paper *Caring for People Five Years On* shows that the reduction in the number of households in receipt of home care between 1992 and 1997 and the increase in the number of hours per household has resulted in a more intensive service for users. The costs, however, include less attention to low level services which might prevent later need, costs recently recognised in *Modernising Social Services*. The evidence from intensive studies of services to older people with dementia would suggest that social services departments' resources are being increasingly used by long term care of people with intensive needs. Moriarty and Webb (1997) argue that as resources are more effectively directed towards older people with dementia whose need for care is intensive and long term, the ability of social services departments to offer preventative services will be increasingly reduced.

Criteria for eligibility for community care are increasingly dependent on proving immediate and urgent need, rather than resting on a judgement whether the situation currently maintained could be supported in the long term by less intensive services. As the Department of Health paper for the Royal Commission on Long Term Care reports, the evidence is so far equivocal on this. We should therefore pause before portraying more intensive services to fewer users as a success, until we can assess whether lower level services have been removed from or denied to other service users and to family carers, with the result that they may at some future stage find themselves facing difficulties that could have been averted.

Needs-led assessment

Needs-led assessment was another key part of the new arrangements for community care. Although clothed in the guise of enhancing consumer choice, needs-led assessment was equally important in the sense of limiting public expenditure to available resources according to criteria laid down locally by the social services department. The assessment process, for example, was firmly under the control of the professional, not of the service user. It is doubtful whether *An agenda for action* was ever underpinned by a genuine understanding of the complexity of social care.

For example, the process of assessment was described as one which
might be 'overseen' by the care manager rather than one which inherently
required the skills and knowledge of the care manager. Need was also
portrayed as an objective fact, as though its existence is unquestionable
and obvious, and simply required to be noted and acted upon by the
professional. The concept that social need is negotiated, that the political
context for defining need might be influential, or that service users might
themselves wish to define their own need, are not areas of which the report
showed any awareness, nor was there any recognition of social policy
thinking about the 'taxonomy' of need, which highlighted the importance of
the context for defining so called 'normative' need (see Sue Balloch's
discussion of identifying need in Chapter 3).

> **'Who defines what the outcomes are?'**
> Comment made at the 19th January seminar

Further, it is doubtful whether the concept of needs-led assessment
represented anything new in front line practice: certainly it emphasised that
people's needs should be central, and that service availability should not
dictate what was offered to service users, but this echoes what
practitioners had been saying all along. Since the legislation, there has
been more opportunity to move away from the concept of professionally
controlled assessment, and self assessment by service users will be an
increasingly important feature of community care services.

Another area of assessment of need inadequately addressed in the new
arrangements for community care concerns service users who may be
resistant to assessment, or who may carefully edit the evidence they give
to an assessor, in case it is used in ways that they would prefer it were not.
For example, older people may not wish to reveal to an assessor the extent
of their difficulties in coping at home, in case the assessor suggests that
they should no longer remain there. Similarly, people with mental health
problems may wish to be extremely careful about what they tell the
assessor. It is not, therefore, just that needs-led assessment is nothing new
in social care, but also that it is infinitely more complex than the architects
of community care allowed.

This is not of course to say that the existing arrangements for assessing
need before the NHS and Community Care Act 1990 were beyond
improvement, nor that needs-led assessment as a concept does not have
the potential to ensure that greater attention is given to the views of the
service user. However, the potential for needs-led assessment to fulfil this
empowering function was considerably reduced when the Gloucestershire
judgement drew attention to the legal obligation on social services
departments to meet need if it had been identified. The incentive to identify
need was constrained by the incentive to reduce the costs of meeting

those needs, until the Lords' judgement that cost could also be taken into account relieved this dilemma.

An example of the potential of placing users' views at the centre of negotiations is whether the need for social participation is recognised as one which social services departments should meet. One of the great successes of the disability movement in implementing independent living and now direct payment schemes has been to ensure that the need for social participation is recognised. Clearly this development, and its links with the underpinning concept of citizenship as a basis for services, could usefully be extended to other groups of service users in community care.

> *'Assessment should take into consideration the rights of social participation of the individual.'*
> Comment made at the 19th January seminar

Care management, social work and social care practice

Care management was intended to be the practice model underpinning the new arrangements for community care. As a concept it derives from the North American welfare system, where it is intended to convey a different role for practitioners, concentrating more on helping users to identify needs and brokering access to services than on directly providing care. In the UK, no specific model of care management was recommended and departments were free to develop models most suited to their needs.

It seems that there have been two positive outcomes of the introduction of care management. First, it is likely that it drew attention to the need to involve skilled professionals in the assessment of community care service users, in the context where departments often did not allocate a substantial proportion of their qualified staff to services to adults. Older people in particular may have benefited from the influx of qualified staff into the assessment and care management role. The second benefit, most recently described by Levin and Webb (1997), was that care management gave added focus and structure to a field where coherent practice models had been lacking. As with needs-led assessment, however, it would be wrong to assume that the skills required of care managers were in any sense new: what was new was the structured system within which existing skills were deployed.

The disbenefits of the introduction of care management may, however, be equally significant. The implication that the care manager had less of a direct role in services is highly problematic: it was often the care manager who possessed the greatest skills to ensure that the service user gained most benefit from the services. For example, an assessment that day care would be an appropriate service must often be matched by careful counselling to assist the user, and sometimes the user's relatives, to gain maximum benefit. This debate has raged in the North American literature on care management for the last decade, with a growing consensus that the care manager should retain a level of involvement designed to assist service users to meet their needs through the services planned.

A second major issue concerns the extent to which care managers were intended to assist service users to navigate the wide variety of service providers it was anticipated that the new arrangements for community care would instigate. Again, there is extensive debate on this in the North American literature, particularly in relation to older people. Ten years ago, Callahan (1989) reported that few service users over the age of 65 used multiple services; only 7% used two services and only 2.7% used three or more. He also quotes evidence from studies of people with mental health problems which show that the average number of services in which a client was enrolled was 1.6. A recent study in the UK by Moriarty and Webb (1997) showed that, of older people with dementia referred to social services eligible for five key services, 74% received two or fewer services. Only one person had a care package consisting of all five. This research suggests that there is a rather limited role for the care manager in guiding at least this group of older service users through the range of services available. If indeed there is little variety in providers, despite the intention to promote a flourishing independent sector, we have to question whether the amount of training and education undertaken to superimpose care management roles on to the existing functions of social workers and home care staff has been worthwhile: Challis has described this situation as increasing the 'overhead' of community care without increasing the benefits (Challis, 1994 p.10).

There has never been sufficient clarity about the practice model underpinning care management, about which staff already possess the required skills or about the appropriate training and education required to develop such skills. The absence of this essential development work has probably lead to a diversification of models which renders analysis of the results of implementing care management practice impossible. What is required is a clear reassessment of the skills required for all of the tasks in community care, and to use this to explore whether the concept of care management and its distinct skills continues to have a role.

Health and social care: collaboration or conflict?

The new arrangements for community care rightly identified the interface between health and social care agencies as the key, a perspective recently reiterated by the Royal Commission on Long Term Care. The artificial division between agencies funded and controlled locally to promote social care and those funded and controlled centrally to promote health care had already proved impervious to the incentives of joint finance, and have subsequently proved to be a continuing source of difficulty. The policy approach to securing better collaboration between health and social care was evidenced in a stream of guidance, key tasks and work books. The objective was 'a shared vision'. Social services as the lead agency has suffered from chronic under investment in management and in information technology, with the result that it was grappling with a health service with more managers equipped with better quality information. These structural disparities continually influence the key issue under debate, namely what is to be defined as health care and what as social care.

Much of this analysis and resulting policy was originally directed at ensuring better collaboration between the hospital sector and social services in the area of continuing care (hence the emphasis in key tasks on discharge arrangements). In essence, this has simply failed, as is evidenced in the widespread redefinition of responsibilities formerly held by health authorities as social care, particularly long term care in non-acute illness and domiciliary care involvement in basic hygiene and nutrition. 'Cost shunting' arises predictably and directly from the financial structure of long term care, and should not be thought of as an aberration on the part of health service managers. Hence the call by the Royal Commission on Long Term Care for shared budgets. In the latter half of the 1990s, the issue has of course moved on from the hospital/social services interface to the primary care/social care interface with the advent of primary care commissioning groups. Although this does not remove continuing care and discharge arrangements from the collaboration agenda, these issues will become much less important in comparison with the need to promote interdisciplinarity in the front line in health and social care assessment. In the context of previous failure, it seems unlikely that the 'duty of partnership' will provide the breakthrough sought.

As the importance of professional factors in front line working becomes recognised, we will need to pay much greater attention to the extent to which social and health care practitioners share both a vision and values. In these circumstances, social services departments are in a position to offer leadership on such issues as user involvement and empowerment.

> *'The social model of disability is not really understood in health as the professionals don't think it applies to them.'*
> Comment made at the 19th January seminar

However, the responsibility on social care agencies to promote independent decision making can sometimes lead to direct conflict with health care providers more accustomed to a model of professional rather than consumer dominance. Forceful advocacy for a particular course of action because it is in the 'patient's' best interests will increasingly be in contrast with a philosophy of participative decision making and self determination. These issues at the professional level will in turn be reflected in structural relations. For example, negotiations about block provision of services or about the 'placement' of future numbers of service users in the community will need to be infused by a thorough recognition of the role of social services to promote choice and active decision making.

This section draws on the following sources:

Baldock, J. (1997) 'Social care in old age: more than a funding problem', *Social Policy and Administration*, 31, 1, p.73-89.

Balloch, S., McLean, J. and Fisher, M. (eds.) (1999) *Social Services: Working under pressure*, Bristol: Policy Press.

Callahan, J. (1989) 'Case management for the elderly: a panacea?', *Journal of Aging and Social Policy*, 1, 1/2, p.181-195.

Challis, D. (1994) *Implementing Caring for People: Care management: factors influencing its development in the implementation of community care*, London: Department of Health.

Clark, H., Dyer, S. and Horwood, J. (1998) *'That Bit of Help': The high value of low level preventative services for older people*, Bristol: Policy Press.

Department of Health (1988) *Community Care: An agenda for action* (The Griffiths Report), London: HMSO.

Department of Health (1991) *Implementing Community Care: Purchaser, commissioner and provider roles*, London: HMSO.

Department of Health (1995) *Carers (Recognition and Services) Act,* London: HMSO.

Department of Health (1998) *Caring for People Five Years On*, paper prepared for the Royal Commission on Long Term Care.

Department of Health (1999) Scoping Study Committee, draft outline proposals.

Doyal, L. (1993) 'Human need and the moral right to optimal community care', in *Community Care: A Reader,* J. Bornat et al. (eds.), Basingstoke: Macmillan, p.276-86.

Dunleavy, P. and Hood, C. (1994) 'From old public administration to new public management', *Public Money and Management*, July-September, p.9-16.

Ermisch, J. (1990) *Fewer Babies, Longer Lives*, York: Joseph Rowntree Foundation.

Fernando, S., Ndegwa, D. and Wilson, M. (1998) *Forensic Psychiatry, Race and Culture*, London: Routledge.

Jack, R. (1991) 'Social services and the ageing population', *Social Policy and Administration*, 25, 4, p. 284-99.

Levin, E. and Webb, S. (1997) *Social Work and Community Care: Changing roles and tasks*, London: NISW.

Lewis, J. and Glennerster, H. (1996) *Implementing the New Community Care*, Buckingham: Open University Press.

Local Government Information Unit (1997) *Splitting the Difference: A consultation paper on the purchaser/provider split in the home care service*, London: LGIU.

Mirza, K. (1991) 'Community care for the black community - waiting for guidance', in *One Small Step Towards Racial Justice: The teaching of anti-racism in diploma in social work programmes,* Paper 8, CCETSW (ed.) London: CCETSW, p.120-146.

Moriarty, J. and Webb, S. (1997) *Part of Their Lives: An evaluation of community care arrangements for older people with dementia*, London: NISW Research Unit.

Royal Commission on Long Term Care (1999) *With Respect to Old Age: Long term care – rights and responsibilities*, Cm.4192, London: The Stationery Office.

Tinker, A. (1984) *The Elderly in Modern Society*, London: Longman.

Twigg, J. (1997) 'Deconstructing the 'social bath': help with bathing at home for older and disabled people', *Journal of Social Policy*, 26, 2, p. 211-232.

Chapter 3

Identifying need

Sue Balloch

Need and demand

At the end of September 1997 the Local Government Management Board (LGMB) recorded a total of 796,000 adults over the age of 65 being supported by their local authorities in residential or nursing homes or in domiciliary care in England and Wales. On average local authorities were providing services to about 96 out of every 1,000 people, or just under 10% of their local over 65 populations. Such figures could be taken as an indication of the average level of need in this population, although they do not include the much lower numbers of those individuals paying for their own care or those of a younger age, nor those being cared for 'informally' by relatives and friends. In the preceding six months (March to September 1997) the LGMB figures showed people supported in residential and nursing care had increased by 3%, while those receiving domiciliary care had dropped by 2%. If we were to assume that the former increase indicated an increase in need while the latter showed a decrease in need, we would be quickly contradicted by evidence from both user groups and research illustrating the shortfall in domiciliary services. In other words, while local authority statistics can give us some idea of prevailing needs, they themselves are the products of policies which do not necessarily reflect the real levels of need in populations.

To plan for community care services in both the short and long term requires predictors of need. Usually predictors are based on knowledge of how different populations use services. For example, older people over 65 are the main users of both residential and domiciliary community care services. Between 1981 and 1997, although the total population of the UK increased by just 5%, those aged between 75 and 84 increased by 18% and those over 85 increased by 80%. Growth of these groups will be slower till 2011 and then will accelerate in the period after 2020. By the middle of the next century there will be 500% more people aged over 85 in the population and so, it is thought, there will be a corresponding increase in pressure on services. Defining needs in terms of demand for services is, however, a practice fraught with problems: existing services may not meet needs as people want; other types of services, yet to be developed, might meet needs much more effectively. The presence of vulnerability does not tell us what services to provide.

The transfer of responsibility for paying for residential and nursing care to local authority social services was to be supported by more rational service planning, including assessments of need, both of individuals and in the wider population. These assessments were to be used in the development of the community care plans which each local authority is required to produce on an annual basis. Local authorities were urged to plan strategically and Price Waterhouse prepared a series of guides for the Department of Health to show how this was to be done. It was clear from the outset, however, that the analysis of any concept of need would be severely circumscribed in a cash-limited context and that strategic planning would be hampered by lack of joint working between social services departments and health and housing agencies.

The legislation discouraged local authorities from recording 'unmet need' because doing so would lay them open to legal challenge from those assessed with needs that the local authority would not or could not meet. Later, the final judgement in favour of Gloucester County Council, mentioned in Chapter 2, made it clear that while local authorities should act reasonably, they could not be expected to meet needs for which their resources were inadequate. Thus there is still little incentive for local authorities to identify unmet need.

In a taxonomy of need developed by Bradshaw (1972) four categories of need were identified: 'normative need' as defined by professionals and experts; 'expressed need' or 'demand' from actual or potential service users; 'felt' need or 'wants' existing in the population; and 'comparative' need in which people are thought to be in need if they suffer the same conditions as others receiving a service but do not receive a service themselves.

Local authorities have tended to concentrate either on 'normative need', that is need as assessed by professionals and experts, or, when mapping the supply side, on 'expressed need' or demand. 'Mapping the market' has become a serious activity for a few. Laing and Buisson produce annual surveys of the market for nursing and residential beds, for example, and a wide range of related statistics. Some local authorities produce their own reports - such as the 'market mapping partnership' in Shropshire. One critic has argued that:

> 'Notwithstanding the accumulation of experience at local level since the implementation of care in the community in 1993... social services departments will have to develop significantly improved bases of information and intelligence about supply and demand for community care in each sector.'

What seems to have been overlooked is the fact that few authorities have paid much attention to 'felt need', a broader and more complex subject, best understood in terms of the gap between a person's or group's current situation and desired outcomes; their preferred outcomes may or may not be expressed, depending on the degree of empowerment and confidence of the individual or group and access to channels of communication with authorities.

Number crunching

Knowledge of local needs was at a low level in most authorities when the 1990 Act was implemented. In a survey of 80 community care plans, Francis McGlone (1993) found little evidence of strategic planning based on either national or local data. Wistow et al. (1997 p.58) comment:

> 'In most authorities, needs mapping in 1993 was still at an early stage of development and was widely regarded as complex, time consuming and costly. Typically, the mapping of needs was restricted to identifying current service utilisation and rarely extended to mapping latent or future needs. Many authorities were still grappling with information systems and technical deficiencies...'

Analysis of 1993/94 community care plans by the above authors showed that nearly half of a sample of 25 authorities (44%) had based their assessments of need solely on basic demographic (OPCS) data. Only 32% had supplemented this with additional sources. Yet local authorities have access to an impressive range of national and local data, including client group registers; current service user referrals; waiting lists; annual public health reports; the General Household Survey; prevalence data from health authorities; DoH key indicators; OPCS disability surveys; Jarman and Townsend deprivation indices; Department of Employment Z scores; and information from their own records on housing benefit, council tax payments and rebates, educational deprivation scores and so forth.

Realising this in the 1980s, a handful of authorities began to build up poverty profiles, such as 'Breadline Greenwich' (1984), 'A Social Atlas of Poverty in Lewisham' (1989), but while these could be used to target services on deprived communities, they were not normally seen as planning tools for social services departments. A few authorities with more advanced IT capabilities introduced the use of GIS (Geographical Information Systems) and in some areas, such as the North West, formed groups of experts to share and develop planning information.

While developing its anti-poverty strategy, one local authority, Newcastle City Council, used such data to reorganise its home care service. The total home care budget for 1992/93 was redistributed between Newcastle's six social services areas on the basis of a formula derived from population projections from the 1981 census and data from a 1986 citizens survey. This 'formula funding' cut posts in four areas to increase posts in one area that had seen a marked growth in its number of older people. Blackman and Atkinson (1997) argue that such strategies may not achieve the benefits intended: firstly, because they may not create the outcomes people want; and secondly, because you cannot be sure that those who finally receive such targeted services are those with the greatest needs. Newcastle satisfied itself on the latter score, however, using a survey with samples of service users and non-users. This suggested that 'assessments were well targeted on people with high levels of disabling conditions, short or critical interval levels of dependency, or health problems leading to difficulties with home life'. Only 7% of assessed respondents were independent, compared with 41% of non-assessed respondents.

The criticism that such strategies, based on national or local data, may not create the outcomes people want is more serious. Data can only provide a background against which to plan services; it cannot and should not dictate the content of planning without prior consultation with service users.

For example, it is useful to know the age profile of an area, and if the population is ageing faster in one area than another, but this is of little use unless you also know if the people in that area are likely to have poor health and little family or community support. Even then, the sort of services finally provided have to be tailored not just to a group, but to individuals.

Another downside of the Newcastle example is that the analysis of need was based around a service, and the delivery of that service. Understanding need requires finding out what local people want to help them cope with everyday living, rather than finding out who does or does not receive, or wants to receive, a service. For example, some services, such as day centres, have been under attack as an inappropriate way of 'warehousing' people; and an analysis of need in terms of who uses day centres, or is on a waiting list for a day centre, would discount other, possibly more effective, ways of meeting need.

Quantity and quality

In spite of all the difficulties, it is clear that local authorities should take responsibility for the joint planning of community care services with health and housing agencies and this requires an adequate information base. Improvements in available information have made this easier than in the past. For example, the Department of Social Security has recorded the findings of a 100% scan of income support recipients in August 1996 which gives totals of claimants for each ward and is further broken down by pensioners, lone parents, unemployed and a combined disabled and 'other' category. It also records the number of children in each ward with parents/guardians receiving income support. The Local Government Management Board distributes this information to all local authorities. Another development has enabled a local authority to estimate the numbers and characteristics of its elderly population with cognitive disability, or dementia. Its authors describe it as 'a simple software package designed for use by those involved in planning services for the elderly. It can provide a basis for evidence-based health care or social care decisions....'

What most local authorities have yet to do, however, is consult systematically with service users and local voluntary organisations on appropriate ways to measure and meet needs and to assess the scale of unmet need. This qualitative data is as important as the quantitative data discussed above – and, some might argue, more important. The challenge for the future is to find a way to integrate both quantitative and qualitative information so that service users can obtain the outcomes that they want for themselves.

This section draws on the following sources:

Anti-Poverty Matters (1998) 'Measuring poverty matters', *Anti-Poverty Matters*, 17, Summer.

Alcock, P. and Craig, G. (1996) *Anti-Poverty Strategies in Local Authorities,* London: Local Government Management Board.

Balloch, S. and Jones, B. (1990) *Poverty and Anti-Poverty Strategy: The local government response,* London: Association of Metropolitan Authorities.

Blackman, T. and Atkinson, A. (1997) 'Needs targeting and resource allocation in community care', *Policy Studies,* 18, 2, June, p.125-138.

Bradshaw, J. (1972) 'The taxonomy of social need' in G. McLachlan (ed.) *Problems and Progress In Medical Care,* Oxford: Oxford University Press.

Edwards, P. and Mellor, D. (1999) *Community Care Trends 1998 Report: The impact of funding on local authorities*, London: Local Government Management Board.

Ely, M., Melzer, D., Opit, L. and Brayne, C. (1996) 'Estimating the numbers and characteristics of elderly people with cognitive disability in local populations', in *Research, Policy and Planning*, 14, 2.

Jarman, B. (1983) 'Identification of underprivileged areas', *British Medical Journal,* 286, p.1705-1709.

Nocon, A. and Qureshi, H. (1996) *Outcomes of Community Care for Users and Carers,* Buckingham: Open University Press.

McGlone, F. (1993) 'The poverty of planning for community care', *Family Policy Bulletin*, June.

Price Waterhouse/Department of Health (1993) *Implementing Community Care: Population needs assessment good practice guidance,* London: Department of Health.

Townsend, P., Corrigan, P. and Kowarzik, U. (1987) *Poverty and Labour in London,* London: Low Pay Unit.

Turner, M. (1999) *Shaping Our Lives,* Interim and Final Reports, London; NISW Policy Unit.

Waddington, P. (1996) 'Mixing it in the mixed economy', *Research, Policy and Planning,* 14, 1.

Wistow, G., Knapp, M., Hardy, B., Forder, J., Kendall, J., Manning, R. (1997) *Social Care Markets: Progress and prospects,* Buckingham: Open University Press.

Chapter 4

Users' perspectives

Vivien Lindow

Some issues from service user perspectives

The NHS and Community Care Act 1990 with accompanying and subsequent government guidance has had a profound effect on the background against which disabled people are working for a rights-based approach to their support in the community. Public permission to speak out, while not the same as being listened to, has transformed some people's approach to services from dependent to assertive. It has also heightened people's expectations and led to a clearer delineation of demands by disabled people, and enabled many people to articulate (in a variety of formats) their expectations and the failures of community care. There also remain many service users and potential users who have not been reached by the knowledge that they might aspire to an independent life supported by the community.

Many of the developments within the movements of disabled people predate the Act. Organisations of disabled people, including people with learning difficulties and mental health service users, were already developing locally and nationally: notably the British Council of Organisations of Disabled People (now the British Council of Disabled People), People First and Survivors Speak Out. The independent living movement was well under way, though given an impetus by some of the principles of the Act. Pioneering work such as that by Beresford and Croft about citizen involvement in the provision of health and social services had been published. Much written work about 'user involvement' builds on their accounts, often repeating the known principles and practicalities which service managers have often failed to incorporate into their practice.

The debate arising from the disabled people's social model of disability has continued during the life of the Act. While some service developments, such as direct payments, have arisen from a rights-based perspective, much social support is still delivered on the traditional needs-led model of social care. There has been some resistance to the social model of disability, particularly in medical-led community services. Another dilemma that has become central to the rights/needs debate is that of equity of provision. There is much evidence of inequity of service provision geographically and between service user groups, with older disabled citizens' right to community support, for example, being less acknowledged than that of younger disabled adults.

'The medical model still prevails. Why? Despite all the community care available, the medical model doesn't consider the quality of life.'
Comment made at the 19th January seminar

The issue of social inclusiveness has been insufficiently linked to the development of community services. While the Social Exclusion Unit and its activities are part of mainstream government policy, this issue is not yet integral to community service provision. Following the theme of rights-based community support, social participation would then become central to assessment and care management, rather than an occasional add-on. Geographical as well as social inequalities are again involved here: for example, public transport is free to those to whom it is accessible in London whereas it is non-existent in many rural areas.

'Mental health is very central to social exclusion discussions.'
Comment made at the 19th January seminar

Two major criticisms by service users are of the inequalities of access to services caused by charging, and the fact that only the most impaired people are being offered support due to shortage of resources and rationing imposed through levels of care management and care programming.

For mental health service users there is a third objection, that any improvements resulting from the legislation and associated guidance are over-ridden by the Government's various attempts to control people in the community. Supervision registers are to be followed by legislation for compulsory 'treatment' (drugs with dangerous side-effects) in the community. It appears that restraint rather than citizens' rights is becoming the policy for mental health service users.

Qualified successes

User participation in commissioning and providing services has helped to create some imaginative schemes, particularly in the areas of supported housing and employment, and of community support in times of crisis for mental health service users. However, evidence remains of lack of rights (tenancy rights, insecure employment) and instead medical model solutions for the vast majority of community service users.

The growth of organisations of disabled people, including mental health system survivors and people with learning difficulties, has been assisted by statutory organisations' need to consult local service users. While these groups sometimes lack independence, more often independent organisations have developed with activities including supporting people in local consultation exercises. Where groups do lack independence it is often because they have been created to meet the statutory sector's agenda of providing people to take part in 'user involvement'. All such groups need resources to develop their own agendas.

It is not known how geographically complete is the coverage by these organisations, but there are certainly hundreds of local organisations of disabled people, psychiatric system survivors, older people, people with learning difficulties and people living with HIV/AIDS. Such groups have not generally received resources to enable them to reach out to the most marginalised people in their constituencies: this includes particularly older elderly people and people who do not communicate with speech. Much more has still to happen to enable disabled people from minority ethnic communities to meet together and, if they wish to join, to feel safe in integrated organisations of disabled people.

Despite these limitations, where organisations of service users have been resourced to develop, many successes can be celebrated. Joining self advocacy organisations can transform the attitudes and goals of members through processes such as understanding the social model of disability, meeting empowered and successful role models and becoming an equal member of a lively democratic organisation.   Some of these organisations have made great strides in getting direct payment and other independent living schemes into action as well as providing advocacy and other user-controlled services. However, these schemes are not available everywhere, and certainly do not extend to all service users who might choose to take part.

Independent advocacy schemes have grown up alongside organisations of disabled people, sometimes as part of them. When they work well, the processes of care management and assessment have improved the lives of service users. Too often, though, this only happens with the assistance of an independent advocate. And once again, the benefit of peer advocacy is limited by local quirkiness in the purchasing and providing mechanisms. The difficulty that disabled people have in accessing resources to form their own organisations and provide services including advocacy is likely to increase as GPs become major purchasers alongside social services and health authorities.

In conclusion, when writing about the successes of community care from a user perspective, they have to be qualified by major failings. First, that examples of good practice are geographically patchy. Second, that examples of good practice seldom reach more marginalised service users, particularly those that do not communicate in the language of statutory commissioners and providers, for reasons of class, circumstance or impairment. Mental health service users have lost many of the advantages they might have received by controlling practices and this will be worse after planned legislation. Third, that the ethnic and cultural diversity of society is not recognised in arrangements for the support of disabled people in the community and for consultation and participation in commissioning and providing services.

Hot issues

Theory and practice

The social model of disability is the preferred model of many disabled people, who perceive themselves to be disabled by the barriers set up in society rather than by their impairments. There has not been the opportunity to explain this model to sufficient numbers of disabled people, commissioners or service providers. It remains contested or neglected in the provision of many community services. Mental health services are among those especially likely to be caught in the determinism of the medical model.

> 'The social model of disability is not really understood in health as the professionals don't think it applies to them.'
> Comment made at the 19th January seminar

Warehousing

Decarceration of service users from the traditional warehouses of the asylums and workhouse based arrangements for older people has not always led to an ordinary life. New forms of warehousing, in residential homes and even in people's own homes, when insufficient support is provided to enable an independent life, are becoming the norm due to insufficient resources. However, the bulk of research findings on the views of former long term patients shows a marked preference for living outside hospital. Planned new money for mental health services is likely to be spent on new forms of institutional 'care', including twenty-four hour nursed beds, reversing the trend towards more independent lives for this group of service users.

> 'For funding reasons people in residential care get £14 per week, making a mockery of independent living.'
> Comment made at the 19th January seminar

Parenting

Disabled people's right to be parents provides areas of conflict in two particular ways. One is the difficulty that disabled people (including people with learning difficulties and mental health service users) have in opposing moves to take their children into care. Instead of viewing people as having the right to be parents and to be given sufficient support to carry out this role, social services often view the situation as one of child protection and consider it to be their duty to deprive children and parents of each other.

The issue of 'young carers' is similarly approached from the perspective of vulnerable children instead of that of the right of disabled parents to sufficient support to enable their offspring to have ordinary childhoods. The fate of young disabled children has also not improved as much as many had hoped at the introduction of the community care legislation.

'Carers'

The term 'carer' is considered by many disabled people to be demeaning, denying the mutuality of most family relationships. A separation of thinking is needed between the everyday mutual support within households and the additional support needs that make one or more members into users of community care services. Using a rights-based approach, the service user should have the right to be an ordinary member of the family by having the resources to get their support needs met.

> **'Carers are constructed as at the heart of things by legislation, but significantly not by users.'**
> Comment made at the 19th January seminar

The tendency of many statutory sector managers to treat service users and 'carers' as having identical interests denies the real conflict of interest that often exist between the two groups. At a collective level organisations of 'carers' often have demands at odds with organisations of disabled people. The call to have attendance allowance paid directly to the family member, not the disabled person, is an example. Within individual families, also, interests can be at odds. For example, the disabled person may wish to have respite at home from their relative, who may wish the disabled person to go away so they may have respite at home.

Racism

Despite much effort, individual and institutional racism still exists in many parts of the community service system. Statistics relating to black and Asian people in the mental health system are particularly illuminating on this point. The voices of black and Asian service users are often not heard because of the expectation that they will be represented by predominately white organisations of disabled people, which may not be safe for them. Black voluntary sector workers are also often accepted as proxies for black service users during consultation and participation exercises.

Control

In the rhetoric of community care, the tensions between supporting independence and providing statutory control functions is often glossed over. Issues relating to parenting have been mentioned.

The lack of community alternatives often leads to the forced use of hospital for mental health service users. The current review of mental health legislation includes a Government pledge to force 'treatment' on people outside hospital. Many of these changes are taking place without the voices of those most concerned being heard: people in the 'forensic psychiatry' system are seldom directly represented. Government policy is being led by a major press campaign that ignores the complexity of the situation, and appears to be scapegoating mental health service users for the general rise in violence in society.

Information

Informed consumers are essential to a rights-based system. Requests for information about the range of choices are a consistent research finding among users of community care services. Where such information is lacking people are dependent on professionals' judgements about their needs and how best to meet them, thus denying service users control over their own lives. Where information is available, it is sometimes not available in the formats and languages that would make it accessible to all service users and potential users.

> **'Everyone needs information.'**
> Comment made at the 19th January seminar

Unheard groups

There are many people who remain almost wholly marginalised. The community care needs of travellers are almost unknown: a literature search brought up only health care issues, not social care. Also barely represented are homeless people and refugees; there has been a decline in the voices of HIV positive people, and some of the innovations in services pioneered by people with AIDS are in danger of being lost. The voices of people in prison in relation to their community support needs are virtually unheard. There will be other groups so neglected that they are not in the consciousness of this writer.

> **'What about those who don't fit into boxes?'**
> Comment made at the 19th January seminar

Social exclusion

Despite the rhetoric of anti-discrimination in the provision of community services, some groups are facing even greater discrimination in wider society. Mental health service users and refugees stand out in this category. If community services do not address this increased prejudice and discrimination, in their own practice and more directly in statements and actions rejecting media representations, they fail.

Community service technicalities

Limitations to direct payment systems

Direct payments, where they have become available to people since April 1997, are one of the successes of recent Government policy from the point of view of disabled people. However, they do not extend to all citizens who might be eligible. Compared to other European countries, direct payment schemes here are rare and inequitable in their reach. Although some extensions to eligible age groups have been announced, without additional funds the schemes are unlikely to reach the most marginalised service users.

> **'Direct payment recipients should be allowed to pay their family members for the assistance they need.'**
> Comment made at the 19th January seminar

A further debate is needed about whether disabled people can use direct payments to pay members of their own households and families. Many disabled people want this option, feeling that the advantages in increased autonomy would outweigh any disadvantages. It would certainly be preferable to paying Government-designated 'carers' directly, as this removes choice and control from the disabled person.

Assessment, care management and the care programme approach

There are reports of assessment and care management working well, but also of its unsatisfactory nature in many cases:

> 'Disabled people and carers found assessment encounters with local authority social service departments confusing, fragmentary and often irrelevant to their own concerns and priorities.'

(JRF Findings, 318)

Resources for the development of self-assessment systems that can be incorporated into community service delivery systems are needed.

Outcomes of community services

Michael Turner, writing as part of the Shaping Our Lives project, has noted that the effect of user involvement on thinking about outcomes of community services has been negligible. Reviewing the literature, he notes that most recent outcome work reflects a medical model, relating to functional ability or mental states rather than quality of life in the community.

Turner suggests that a major development project by disabled people is needed to discover outcome measures in terms of the removal of physical and social barriers, rather than the values and goals of the service providers that inform most current outcome measures. Such a project would include the full diversity of communities and disabled people, and outcome measures would need to be flexible, person-centred and include subjective elements.

> 'Need, like vulnerability, is not a given thing: it is to do with the lack of support around you.'
> Comment made at the 19th January seminar

While a great deal more is now known about what service users want from community support services, personal reports and collective reports of user views remain under valued by planners and providers. It is only when the culture of planning and policy making changes to regard service users as expert witnesses that user defined outcome measures will take their place in informing service provision.

Service users as researchers

Research by disabled people is a growing field, but as with so much related to the NHS and Community Care Act this trend has developed in a geographically piecemeal fashion. User research seldom includes the most marginalised service users as researchers, although user researchers themselves attempt to reach these groups. Most research resources in this field are arbitrated by medical practitioners, leaving user research marginalised in funding and in prestige. Black and minority ethnic service users are similarly often dependent on white filtered and/or professional filtered research into issues of concern to them.

> 'Who defines what the outcomes are?'
> Comment made at the 19th January seminar

User evaluations of aspects of services have become much more common and often provide an impetus for change, usually in small scale ways. However, where more powerful stakeholders oppose user-led demands, user accounts are in general subordinated. This applies most often at national and regional policy making levels.

Service users as educators

Again, training by service users is piecemeal by geographical area and by the group of service users concerned. Disability equality training has become accepted on basic professional courses and as in-service training in many areas. There are local and national initiatives such as the CCETSW supported user controlled initiative to take forward user involvement in social care education.

Generally, though, training provided by service users remains an add-on to traditional forms of education rather than a part of curricula devised with service users as equal stakeholders in planning their design. Many providers of services remain untouched by the social model of disability, the Disability Discrimination Act and even the potential of the NHS and Community Care Act.

Service user educators and trainers need to be drawn more widely from all parts of the service using constituencies. This will involve providing resources to enlarge the pool of trainers.

The workforce

An allied question arising from a rights-based approach to community support is that of whether the professional groupings as they are now configured are useful for a modern community support system. Many disabled people report that they prefer to train personal assistants themselves so that tasks are done to their satisfaction and convenience. There is evidence that some mental health service users benefit from and prefer untrained fellow-citizens assisting them with their daily lives to more expensive professional interventions. The disappearance of the home help system, highly valued by service users, especially elderly citizens, flies in the face of such practical preferences about the form that community support should take.

These developments obviously challenge the autonomy of professional groups. The reshaping of community services may mean over-riding some professional demarcation lines and self protective measures.

Disabled people as workers in community services

Another key issue is the accessibility of professional training to disabled people to enable them to take their place in the community service workforce. While there is some improvement on some courses, mental health system survivors report disadvantages of having past service use known on courses and in employment in community services. Accessibility for people with different impairments is patchy, both in training and in work opportunities.

User participation

Large numbers of users have worked very hard to service the services that are supposed to serve them since before the NHS and Community Care Act. In some places, such as Wiltshire, the Act has prompted social services departments to fund service user groups and they have benefited from the talents and expertise of their users. Sometimes this work has been successful in changing aspects of community care, but purchasers and providers have often resisted the changes in organisation culture and working practices that would enable experts in using services to contribute fully to improving those services. Disabled people have often been frustrated by limited results of user involvement, where it happens, leading to 'involvement fatigue'. There are signs that user involvement has now lost its flavour of the month status.

A continuing insult to service users who take part in user involvement is the suggestion that they are not representative. This usually occurs when the other (unrepresentative) statutory sector workers involved in the consultation exercise do not like what the service users are saying and wish to discount it. It is a major culture change for many workers to overcome such 'clientism' and accept service users as equal on such occasions. This is a different issue from the obligation of service commissioners and providers to make sure they consult a broad range of service users.

Despite the massive growth of user participation in planning and provision of community services, the same qualifications that apply to other aspects of community care apply to user participation. Payment of service users for sharing their expertise with purchasers and providers has become more common, though it is by no means universal. The lumping together of 'users-and-carers' as though they were a common interest group remains in some NHS trusts and social services departments. Extending representation to service users whom managers find hard to reach is as unsatisfactory in user participation as it is in other areas of community care.

Since there are now detailed coherent guidelines for involvement produced by service users and others, there is no excuse for the continuing failure in community care generally to involve people equally and effectively. We know how to do it properly.

This section draws on the following sources:

Bamford, C., Vernon, A., Nicholas, E. and Qureshi, H. (1998) *Outcomes for Younger Disabled People and Their Carers,* Report to Department of Health (DH 1606), York: Social Policy Research Unit, University of York.

Begum, N., Hill, M. and Stevens, A. (1994) *Reflections: The views of black disabled people on their lives and community care*, London: CCETSW.

Beresford, P. (1997) 'The last social division? revisiting the relationship between social policy, its producers and consumers', *Social Policy Review*, 9.

Beresford, P. and Turner, M. (1997) *It's Our Welfare: Report of the Citizens' Commission on the Future of the Welfare State,* London: National Institute for Social Work.

Beresford, P. and Campbell, J. (1994) 'Disabled people, service users, user involvement and representation', *Disability and Society*, 9, 3, p.315-325.

Beresford, P. and Croft, S. (1993) *Citizen Involvement: A practical guide for change*, Basingstoke: Macmillan.

Beresford, P. and Harding, T. (eds.) (1993) *A Challenge to Change: Practical experiences of building user-led services*, London: National Institute for Social Work.

Berrington, E., Cartwright, L. and Johnstone, D. (1996) *The People Factor: The lives and circumstances of disabled people in West Lancashire 1993-96* (2 volumes), West Lancashire: West Lancashire Association for Disabled People/Edge Hill University College.

Bewley, C. and Glendinning, C. (1994) *Representing the Views of Disabled People in Community Care Planing,* York: Joseph Rowntree Foundation.

Beeforth, M., Conlan, E. and Graley, R. (1994) *Have We Got Views for You: User evaluation of case management*, London: Sainsbury Centre for Mental Health.

Campbell, J. and Oliver, M. (1996) *Disability Politics: Understanding our past, changing our future*, London: Routledge.

Crepaz-Keay, D., Binns, C. and Wilson, E. (1997) *Dancing with Angels: Involving survivors in mental health training*, London: CCETSW.

Crisis Point 1-6: Practical information on all aspects of mental health services, London: Mental Health Foundation.

Croft, S. and Beresford, P. (1993) *Getting Involved: A practical manual*, London: Open Services Project.

Evans, C. (1997) *From Bobble Hats to Red Jackets*, Swindon: Wiltshire and Swindon Users' Network.

Evans, C. (1996) 'From those who know: the role of service users', in C. Hanvey and T. Philpot (eds) *Sweet Charity*, London: Routledge, p.69-81.

Evans, C. (1996) 'Service users as agents of change', in P. Bywaters and E. McLeod (eds) *Working for Equality in Health,* London: Routledge, p.81-93.

Evans, C. (1993) *Tall Oaks from Little Acorns: The Wiltshire experience of involving users in the training of professionals in care management*, Swindon: Wiltshire Social Services/Wiltshire Users' Network.

Faulkner, A. (1997) *Knowing Our Own Minds: A survey of how people in mental distress take control of their lives,* London: Mental Health Foundation.

Fernando, S., Ndegwa, D. and Wilson, M. (1998) *Forensic Psychiatry, Race and Culture*, London: Routledge.

Fernando, S. (ed.) (1995) *Mental Health in a Multi-ethnic Society: A multi-disciplinary handbook*, London: Routledge.

Hastings, M. and Crepaz-Keay, D. (1995) *The Survivors' Guide to Training Approved Social Workers*, London: CCETSW.

Hawcroft, L., Peckford, B. and Thomson, A. (1995) *Visible Voices: Developing deaf service user involvement in local services*, Coventry: British Deaf Association.

Joseph Rowntree Foundation Findings:

- Evaluation of the National User Involvement Project, 129, January 1999.

- Supporting people with mental health problems in ordinary housing, 948, September 1998.

- Deaf people from minority ethnic groups: initiatives and services, 818, August 1998.

- The effectiveness of a local community care rights project, 828, August 1998.

- Access to assessment: the perspectives of practitioners, disabled people and carers, 318, March 1998.

- Involving users and carers in the care programme approach in mental health, SCR 97, October 1997.

- Housing, support and the rights of people with learning difficulties, SCR 81, March 1996.

- Housing choices and community care, HR 168, February 1996.

Lindow, V. (1996) *User Involvement: Community service users as consultants and trainers*, Leeds: Department of Health.

Lindow, V. and Morris, J. (1995) *Service User Involvement: Synthesis of findings and experience in the field of community care*, York: Joseph Rowntree Foundation.

Maglajlic, R., Bryant, M., Brandon, D. and Given, D. (1998) 'Direct payments in mental health – a research report', *Breakthrough*, 2, 3, p.33-43.

Morris, J. (1995) *Gone Missing: A research and policy review of disabled children living away from their families*, London: Who Cares? Trust.

Morris, J. (1994) *The Shape of Things to Come? User-led social services,* Social Services Policy Forum Paper No. 3, London: National Institute for Social Work.

Morris, J. (1993) *Community Care or Independent Living?*, York: Joseph Rowntree Foundation.

NISW Briefing: Shaping futures – rights, welfare and personal social services, 24, June 1998.

O'Neil, A. and Statham, D. (eds.) (1998) *Shaping Futures: Rights, welfare and personal social services,* London: National Institute for Social Work/Joseph Rowntree Foundation.

Reeves, A. (1998) 'Skallagrigg House', *Crisis Point*, 5, p.2-3.

Repper, J., Sayce, L., Strong, S., Willmot, J. and Haines, M. (1997) *Tall Stories from the Back Yard: A survey of NIMBY opposition to community mental health facilities, experienced by key service providers in England and Wales*, London: Mind Publications.

Rooke-Matthews, S. and Lindow, V. (1998) *A Survivors' Guide to Working in Mental Health Services,* London: Mind Publications.

Smith, R., Gaster, L., Harrison, L., Martin, L., Means, R. and Thistlethwaite, P. (1993) *Working Together for Better Community Care*, Bristol: SAUS Publications.

Stewart, M. (1997) *Peer Advocacy in Practice: Disabled people's experiences of community care assessment,* Bristol: West of England Centre for Integrated Living.

Turner, M. (1998) *Shaping Our Lives: Literature review*, London: National Institute for Social Work (unpublished).

Turner, M. (ed.) (1998) *It's Our Day: A national user conference*, London: National Institute for Social Work.

Wallcraft, J. (1998) *Healing Minds*, London: Mental Health Foundation.

Wellard, S. (1999) 'The costs of control', *Community Care*, 21 January, p.23.

Wilson, M. and Francis, J. (1997) *Raised Voices: African-Caribbean and African users' views and experiences of mental health services in England and Wales,* London: Mind Publications.

Wiltshire and Swindon Users' Network (1996) *I Am in Control: Research into users' views of the Wiltshire Independent Living Fund*, Devizes: Wiltshire Community Care User Involvement Network.

Chapter 5

The perspectives of black communities

Jabeer Butt

Introduction

Conducting a review of the NHS and Community Care Act 1990 and its impact on the development and delivery of services to black and minority ethnic communities is potentially a daunting task. In part this is due to the Act having wide-ranging implications, from how resources should be targeted, to how practice should develop and change, to who should provide what services, to how users (and potential users) should be involved in services. However, part of the difficulty is that while the present day evidence base has improved significantly, it is nevertheless the case that in 1990 we had little comprehensive research on how community care was supporting Asian, Caribbean and African communities. Furthermore, the reviews of literature that have appeared in the 1990s, while illuminating, have often demonstrated the gap between the research available on the majority population and that available on black and minority ethnic communities. As importantly, in some areas where the Act has had an impact, there is little research evidence to draw upon: for example what, if any, changes have taken place in the financial resources available for services to black communities; or in direct care practice with them? Additionally, the research that has been done says little about smaller communities or those that have migrated more recently. This may in part be because the majority of service development has been for Asian and Caribbean communities; nevertheless it remains a gap in the research.

With these caveats in mind, it is still possible to build up some picture of the developments and changes that have taken place since 1990 in community care services for black communities.

Background

The 1991 Census revealed that Britain's black communities accounted for 5.5% of the total population (just over 3 million people). The largest of these communities (using Census categories) was those of Indian origin and the smallest Chinese. The overall picture showed that black communities continued to be comparatively younger than their white counterparts (with 39% of white people *over* the age of 45, while over 80% of black people were *under* the age of 45). However, it also showed that the number of black people of pensionable age had grown from 61,000 in

1981 to 164,000 in 1991 (a growth of 168%), and the majority of these older people were of Caribbean or Indian origin.

A further feature revealed by the 1991 Census is the continuing clustering of black communities in particular areas. Owen (1994) shows that a large percentage of these communities continue to live in wards where the percentage of black people is four times the national average. This clustering has raised the spectre of black 'ghettos' in Britain. However, it is equally part of the dynamic that has led to and supported community action, resulting in the development of supportive community care services by black voluntary groups (described below).

Our knowledge of the incidence of impairment and the experience of disability amongst black communities is limited. When the proxy of long term limiting illness is used (using data from the 1991 Census) there is evidence of variation between the different black communities, but when standardised for age there appear to be similar rates to those found amongst white people. In contrast, local studies do suggest a higher incidence of impairment, especially amongst older black people. However, a recent investigation of deafness has also reminded us that the 'recruitment process' which was at the heart of migration in the 1950s and 1960s primarily selected the young and fit, to the exclusion of those with impairments. Nevertheless, it is probable that the incidence of impairment is unlikely to be lower amongst black communities.

An investigation of the incidence of mental illness is an inherently complex task. This is more so when the instruments used to assess mental well being encompass concepts of well being and illness that may be foreign to those it is now being applied to. Nazroo (1997), in his attempt to explore incidence of mental illness through a 'community survey', rather than examining the incidence of those who are already receiving 'treatment', presents valuable new data. In particular he casts doubt on whether the Caribbean community as a whole and Caribbean men in particular have higher rates of psychosis. However, his own doubts and those of others about the instruments used in the survey, as well as the frailty of his sample (in overall terms only 33% of Caribbeans and 42% of South Asians responded, in comparison to 46% of whites) suggest at the very least we need to be cautious on the significance of his findings. What we can say safely is that there are black people who are experiencing mental distress who require support from others, including agencies, and that the incidence of this is unlikely to be lower than that for white people.

Community care services for black communities before 1990

The emerging research on black older people in the 1980s showed that while they were present in comparatively small numbers in a few areas in Britain:

- black older people had considerable health and social care needs and that these needs occur for a comparatively younger group of black older people than white older people;

- despite the existence of these care needs, black older people's knowledge and use of services was limited in comparison to white older people;

- there is some evidence that black older people were more likely to face a greater level of poverty and have lower levels of income than white older people;

- black older people were more likely to live in poorer quality housing which lacks basic amenities.

The evidence from these and other studies led Norman (1985) to suggest that black older people found themselves facing 'double jeopardy'.

The pre-1990 research evidence in terms of services to black disabled adults is perhaps more limited than for black older people. However, the information that we can draw upon suggests:

- black disabled people had to contend with discrimination and disadvantage associated with their disability and as a result of racism;

- despite clear evidence of the existence of disability amongst black communities, access to and knowledge of services was low amongst both black disabled people and their carers;

- there is also evidence that effective communication was a barrier for Asian and Caribbean disabled people.

The pre-1990 (and to an extent the post-1990) research on mental illness and black communities is mostly dominated by research on black people in some form of hospital care. The studies that exist vary in their findings as to whether it is first or second generation people of Caribbean origin who are over-represented, or whether it is the young or older people from this community who are over-represented, or whether it is men or women. However:

- they are consistent in showing some form of over-representation of the Caribbean community under a compulsory order, most suggesting that this is particularly so for young men;

- there is further evidence of over-representation in secure units and some suggestion that those held in these units were less likely to have committed serious offences and more likely to have been referred because they had absconded rather than because they were deemed aggressive;

- evidence with regard to the Asian community is contradictory, in that some studies suggest over-representation in admissions, while others suggest rates similar to the English, and still others suggest under-representation;

- in examining access to services and treatment there is some evidence that black people do not have access to counselling services and psychotherapy.

While the mounting evidence of the lack of accessible and appropriate services for black communities in the 1980s suggested that the 'burden' of caring was being met by 'informal carers' from these communities, it is nevertheless the case that there is very little research specifically focussing on this group of black 'users'. The research that exists suggests that:

- just as in the white community, carers in black communities were unsupported and isolated;

- furthermore, just as in the white community, the mainstay of day care was women;

- the lack of support for and isolation of black carers was particularly exacerbated by communication difficulties, the lack of appropriate service provision, greater poverty, bad housing and racism;

- the needs of black carers were numerous, ranging from education on health, diet and care, to support with caring;

- these studies question the myth of 'black people looking after their own'. It appears we confuse the higher proportion of multi-generational households in black communities as evidence of the existence of caring relationships.

Thus the label of 'piecemeal and patchy' that had first been used to describe social services to black communities in the late 1970s was one that appeared to be equally valid for community care services in 1990. As importantly, the evidence suggests that the service context for black people was often different. Firstly, it was not the case that black older people were going into residential care when they could be supported at home. The reality was that Asian and Caribbean older people who needed support were not going into residential accommodation at all. Neither was it the case that black people with mental health problems were being sent to hospital when they could have been diverted into community based services, because often there were no appropriate community services. Furthermore, it can be argued the practice of many of the workers carrying out assessments did not allow them to consider this as a possibility. Finally, where there was evidence of appropriate provision it was often associated with black-led voluntary organisations.

Community care services for black communities after 1990

Research in the period that has followed the passing of the Act has to an extent reinforced the picture of the 1980s studies; the inappropriateness or lack of services for black older people, including some evidence of services being offered and rejected. At the same time there appears to have been a failure to recognise (or diagnose) depression and dementia; a continuing failure to recognise and respond to the needs of Asian carers; and lack of counselling and community based services for those black people with mental health problems, even when there are examples of how services can be developed appropriately and effectively. At the same time there is more evidence of the lack of services for black disabled adults, but this has been accompanied by new evidence that some service developments that have focused on specific needs of Asian disabled people have failed to deliver better services.

However, it must be emphasised that the picture as we approach the year 2000 is not what it was a decade earlier. Virtually all the studies that have identified continuing limitations of service provision in the context of existing needs (and in the context of black older people - a significant growth in the numbers needing services) have also detailed some development in service provision. The growth in numbers of black workers (in the assessment of social care providers an often cited success in itself) does appear to have some impact on the quality of services received. While systematic evidence on the impact of black voluntary sector care providers is still unavailable, it is nevertheless the case that their contribution is increasingly being highlighted, particularly with regard to supportive services. There is evidence of change in mainstream provision also: for example, Johnson et al. (1996) show that the occupational therapy service in one West Midlands authority had a higher than expected number of black people as users and while they had to wait longer for their assessments they were more likely to get what they wanted. At the same time there is evidence that this has been accompanied by change in the health service also.

Expectations of the NHS and Community Care Act 1990

The limited recognition by the Government White Paper *Caring for People* that services needed to meet the needs of 'ethnic minority communities' was not translated into any specific reference in the 1990 Act itself. This was in the face of a concerted campaign by many, including the Race Equality Unit at NISW, to ensure that specific duties would be imposed on local authorities to identify and respond to the needs of black adults who needed support in the community. This failure of the Act appeared to be compounded when the guidance documents began to appear, with many either not mentioning black communities specifically, or only doing so in passing (often with reference to communicating effectively – see the guidance on care management and assessment). While the lack of detail in the policy guidance was explained as the Government's desire not to be 'prescriptive', the lack of detail in the practice guidance was said to be because the Department of Health were going to issue a specific practice guide for 'race and community care'. This situation was particularly worrying as there was evidence that service development for black communities was still marked by confusion as to what was needed to meet the needs of black communities.

These limitations inevitably led to a string of commentators pointing out the possible consequences. There was the suggestion that community care plans would not identify needs, particularly unmet needs of black adults and their carers. It was argued that in developing the mixed economy of care, black voluntary organisations would not be in a position to compete for contracts. The lack of guidance on how care management and assessment should be implemented did not recognise the limits of existing practice, and therefore the requirement to focus on individual needs would lead to stereotypes not being challenged. The focus on individual needs was also challenged, with a suggestion that it meant care providers would not recognise the collective experience of racism and the possibility that some responses had to be community-wide if needs of individuals were to be met satisfactorily. Equally, the focus on more efficient use of resources and the development of contracting did not appear to recognise that there may be various influences on the cost of particular services. For example, it is unlikely that the cost of preparing meals for Caribbean and Asian older people will be the same as for white people, because at the very least economies of scale may not be available.

Stewart (1996) has criticised these commentators, suggesting that they have chosen to focus on the obvious failings and not highlighted a number of the positives. While Stewart does rightly highlight the opportunities offered by the legislation and guidance, he also demonstrates a naivety which stops him recognising the scale of the failure on the part of those framing the legislation and guidance. It must be remembered that the 1990 Act went through Parliament after the Children Act 1989 which had been a 'landmark' Act in actually imposing duties on social care providers to take into account 'race, religion, language and diet'.

The long and tortuous journey of the 'race and community care' guidance perhaps is proof positive that those who worried about the failings of the 1990 Act were right to do so. The race and community care guidance eventually appeared in October 1997, as a CRE/Institute of Housing/AMA document rather than as Department of Health guidance. It had failed to get ministerial approval in the last days of the Conservative Government. It also failed to secure Labour Party approval and therefore the possibility that it might have been issued as Department of Health guidance with 'cross-bench support' was also lost. As a consequence it was published nearly four years after work began and does not have the same status as other DoH community care guidance.

What impact has the NHS and Community Care Act 1990 had?

In this final section we consider whether the NHS Community Care Act has had any impact. Has it supported the development of a needs-based approach to service provision? The rhetoric certainly appears to exist in large amounts if we examine community care plans as well as other pronouncements. In addition, in many areas this has been accompanied by a wide variety of statements on the needs of black people specifically (often in multi-coloured documents). Furthermore, there is clear evidence that a significant number of the services that now exist did not exist before 1990 (sheltered housing in Newham, specific home care services in Camden, support for disabled adults in Leamington Spa). In addition, these services support a more diverse group of people (the Chinese in Liverpool, Asians in Leicester, Caribbeans in Bristol), and they also exist throughout the country (in Southampton, Newcastle, High Wycombe). Nevertheless, the first ever Social Services Inspectorate inspection of community care services for black older people showed that most departments' response was still inadequate.

Has it supported black people in continuing to live independently in the community? In as much as that there are now services such as day care centres (in particular for older people, as well as some for adults with mental health problems or with disabilities); a significant growth in sheltered housing; home care services; some evidence of access to aids and adaptations; counselling services for adults with mental health problems: then the answer is yes, it has. However, this positive response must be placed in the context that pre-1990, and probably today in some areas, the non-existence of these services for black older people, for instance, would not have meant that they went into residential care but that they would have stayed at home and added to the demands on their carers, or died earlier than might have otherwise been the case. Nor does the positive answer mean that the services are adequate or appropriate: the experience of Christopher Clunis, amongst others, is perhaps some evidence of this. Equally, it is not clear that deaths such as those of Beverly Lewis (a young woman with multiple disabilities who was left in the care of her mentally ill mother) will not happen again.

Has it encouraged the development of a mixed economy of care with more independent and private sector providers of services to black communities? With regard to the independent sector, the answer again is yes. However, many would argue that the main impact has been to move grant-funded black organisations to becoming providers of services on some form of contract. There are clearly some organisations for whom this has not been a problem; for many others the process of being prepared to deal with contracts has been a burden in itself, although detailed assessment is still needed. Furthermore, it could be argued that the new providers that have appeared (both registered charities and social companies) would have emerged regardless of the existence of the Act. They have more to do with increasingly articulate communities demanding that their needs be met, as well as 'social entrepreneurs' having the skills and experience to develop such services.

Importantly, there is little evidence to suggest that the worries expressed about the level of resources available to these organisations were unfounded. The research on resources available to black voluntary organisations as a whole continues to be inadequate, and this is also the case for those providing community care services, with some studies choosing not to identify their evidence separately. If the analysis carried out by Butt and Mirza (1997) on funding of black voluntary organisations in London proves to be correct, then the overall growth in funding given to these organisations in the 1990s masks the fact that more black-led organisations are being funded, and therefore while there is more money it is spread more thinly.

Has it encouraged user-led services? Once again the answer has to be a qualified yes. There is clear evidence that in some services there is considerable user involvement. The development of sheltered accommodation for black older people in London, Leicester, Liverpool and elsewhere has been a clear response to black older people identifying how they want to live and be supported. However, it can be said that where black communities are seen to be accessing services there is likely to be a greater degree of user involvement anyway (and this is also true in the few examples of community based mental health services). So where there are accessible services there is greater user involvement, but whether this has been encouraged by the Act is open to question.

Has it had an impact on assessment? If the fact that there are more black people using community care services than before 1990 is a measure, then yes, it has had an impact. However, the research on what change in assessment practice has taken place is particularly limited. Furthermore, we are likely to find that a range of factors has impacted on assessment practice, including more informed and articulate black users; an increase in numbers of black workers; and availability of more appropriate services.

Finally, it is worth noting that the most remarkable change that has taken place is in residential care provision. There has been both a change in the way these services are provided (so existing providers have looked at how to improve their services to black older people) and in the quantity of services (there has been a significant increase in the number of private sector and housing association providers). Explanations as to why this change has taken place, when a major thrust of Government policy is to encourage support to allow people to remain in the community and out of residential provision, have to focus on the changing make-up of black communities (we have three times as many black older people as we did 15 years ago), as well as a growing recognition that if residential care services were appropriate black older people would use them.

Conclusion

It is the case that community care services for black communities in most urban areas have improved since 1990. However, we must place this in the context that black communities continue to live in areas that have been at the forefront of the transformations that have taken place in Britain in the 1980s and 1990s. They are more likely to live in areas with higher unemployment rates and are more likely to experience unemployment in times of economic depression. While out of all black households Pakistani and Bangladeshi households are more likely to have incomes below half the average household income, it is nevertheless the case that all black communities are likely to have higher numbers of households below this measure of poverty than is the case for white households. Black older people continue to live in 'inner city areas' while white older people continue to be over-represented in seaside towns.

A final point to note is that what some of us understood by needs-led services and what may have been understood by those developing the policies and practice that supported the NHS and Community Care Act may not be one and the same thing. A glance at the community care demonstration projects would suggest that many had enshrined within them a 'professional-knows-best' perspective, so you could decide whether you wanted a blue or black car, but not whether you wanted a car at all. Perhaps, if this Government does not loose its nerve and social care providers (particularly social services departments) follow through the logical conclusions of direct payments, then this is where the real (radical) transformation of the provision of support in the community will occur.

This section draws on the following sources:

ADSS/CRE (1978) *Multi-racial Britain: The social services response*, London: Commission for Racial Equality.

Ahmad, W. and Atkin, K. (1996) *Race and Community Care*, Buckingham: Open University Press.

Ahmad, W., Darr, A., Jones, L. and Nisar, G. (1998) *Deafness and Ethnicity: Services, policy and politics*, Bristol: Policy Press.

Atkin, K. and Rollings, J. (1991) *Community Care in a Multi-racial Britain: A critical review of the literature,* London: HMSO.

Atkin, K. and Rollings, J. (1996) 'Looking after their own? Family care giving among Asian and Afro-Caribbean communities', in W. Ahmad and K. Atkin (eds.), *Race and Community Care*, Buckingham: Open University Press.

Atkin, K (1996) 'Voluntary sector provision in a mixed economy of care', in W. Ahmad, and K. Atkin (eds), *Race and Community Care*, Buckingham: Open University Press.

Azmi, S., Hatton, C., Kane, A. and Emerson, E. (1996) *Improving Services for Asian Families with Learning Disabilities: The views of users and carers*, Manchester: Hester Adrian Research Centre.

Baxter, C., Poonia, K. and Ward, L. (1990*) Double Discrimination*, London: Kings Fund Centre/CRE.

Begum, N. (1994) 'Optimism, pessimism and care management: the impact of community care policies', in N. Begum, M. Hill and A. Stevens (eds.), *Reflections: Views of black disabled people on their lives and community care*, London: CCETSW.

Berthoud, R. (1998) *The Incomes of Ethnic Minorities*, ISER Report 98-1, Colchester: University of Essex, Institute for Social and Economic Research.

Berry, S., Lee, M. and Griffiths, S. (1981*) Report and Survey of West Indian Pensioners in Nottingham,* Nottingham: Nottingham Social Services Department.

Bhatnagur, K. and Frank, J. (1997) 'Psychiatric disorders in elderly people from the Indian sub-continent living in Bradford', *International Journal of Geriatric Psychiatry*, 12, p.907-912.

Blakemore, K. (1983) 'Ageing in the inner city: a comparison of old blacks and old whites', in D. Jerome (ed.), *Ageing in Modern Society*, London: Croom Helm.

Bowl, R. and Barnes, M. (1990) 'Race, racism and mental health social work: implications for local authority policy and training', *Research, Policy and Planning*, 18, 2, p.12-18.

Bright, L. and Turay, M. (1996) *More than Black and White*, London: Counsel and Care.

Butt, J., Gorbach, P. and Ahmad, B. (1991) *Equally Fair?,* London: NISW (reprinted by HMSO in 1994).

Butt, J. (1994*) Same Service or Equal Service?,* London: HMSO.

Butt, J. and Mirza, K. (1996) *Social Care and Black Communities*, London: HMSO.

Butt, J. and Box, L. (1997) *Supportive Services, Effective Strategies: The views of black-led organisations and social care agencies on the future of social care for black communities,* London: REU.

Butt, J. and Mirza, K. (1997) 'Exploring the income of black-led voluntary organisations', in C. Pharoah (ed.), *Dimensions of the Voluntary Sector*, London: Charities Aid Foundation.

Cameron, E. et al. (1988*) Black Old Women, Disability and Health Carers*, Birmingham: Health Services Research Centre, University of Birmingham.

Cocking, I. and Athwal, S. (1990) 'A special case for treatment', *Social Work Today*, 21, 22, p.12-13.

Commission for Racial Equality (1989) *Racial Equality in Social Services Departments*, London: CRE.

Confederation of Indian Organisations (1986) *Double Bind: To be disabled and Asian,* London: CIO.

Cope, R. (1989) 'The compulsory detention of Afro-Caribbeans under the Mental Health Act', *New Community*, p.343-356.

Farrah, M. (1986) *Black Elders in Leicester: An action research report on the needs of black elderly people of African descent from the Caribbean*, Leicester: Leicester Social Services Department.

Francis, E. (1991) 'Mental health, anti-racism and social work training', in D. Divine (ed.), *One Small Step Towards Racial Justice,* London: CCETSW.

GLAD (1987) *Disability and Ethnic Minority Communities: A study in three London Boroughs,* London: Greater London Association for Disabled People.

Grimley, M. and Bhat, A. (1989) 'Mental health', in A. Bhat, R. Carr-Hill and S. Ohri (eds.), *Britain's Black Population*, London: Gower.

Gunaratnum, Y. (1990) 'Asian carers', *Carelink,* 11, p.6.

Haskey, J. (1996) 'Population review (5): older people in Great Britain', *Population Trends*, 84.

Hills, J. (1998) *Income and Wealth: The latest evidence*, York: Joseph Rowntree Foundation.

Jones, A. and Phillips, M. (1992) *A Home from Home*, London: National Institute for Social Work.

Johnson, M., Wright, A., Jeffcoat, M., Petherick, R. (1996) 'Local authority occupational therapy services and ethnic minority clients', *British Journal of Occupational Therapy*, 59, 3, p.109-114.

Kendall, J. and Knapp, M. (1996) *The Voluntary Sector in the UK*, Manchester: Manchester University Press.

Lattimer, M. (1992) *Funding Black Groups: A report into the charitable funding of ethnic minority organisations,* London: Directory of Social Change.

Lewando-Hundt, G. and Grant, L. (1987) 'Studies of black elders – an exercise in window dressing or the groundwork for widening provision? Coventry Survey', *Social Services Research* 5 and 6.

McCalman, J. (1990) *The Forgotten People: Carers in three minority ethnic communities in Southwark,* London: Kings Fund Carers Unit.

Mercer, K. (1986) 'Racism and transcultural psychiatry', in P. Miller and N. Rose (eds.), *The Power of Psychiatry*, London: Blackwell.

Mirza, K (1991) 'Community care for the black community – waiting for guidance', in D. Divine (ed.), *One Small Step for Racial Equality,* London: CCETSW.

Murray, U. and Brown, D. (1998) *They Look After Their Own, Don't They? Inspection of Community Care Services for Black and Minority Ethnic Older People*, London: Department of Health.

Nazroo, J. (1997) *The Mental Health of Ethnic Minorities*, London: Policy Studies Institute.

Netto, G. (1996) *'No One Asked Me Before': Addressing the needs of black and minority ethnic carers of older people in Edinburgh and the Lothians,* Glasgow: SEMRU.

Norman, A. (1985) *Triple Jeopardy: Growing old in a second homeland*, Policy Studies in Ageing No.3, London: Centre for Policy on Ageing.

Owen, D. (1994) *Black People in Great Britain: Social and economic circumstances*, Coventry: University of Warwick Centre for Research in Ethnic Relations.

Patel, N. (1990) *A 'Race' Against Time? Social services provision to black elders,* London: Runnymede Trust.

Patel, N., Mirza, N., Lindbald, P., Amstrup, K., Samaoli, O. (1998) *Dementia and Minority Older People,* London: Russell House Publishing.

Pharoah, C. (1995) *Primary Health Care for Elderly People from Black and Minority Ethnic Communities,* London: HMSO.

Poonia, K. and Ward, L. (1990) 'Fair share of the care', *Community Care*, 796, 11 January.

Russell, L., Scott, D. and Wilding, P. (1995) *Mixed Fortunes: The funding of the local voluntary sector,* Manchester: Manchester University Press.

Rait, G. and Burns, A. (1997) 'Appreciating background culture: the South Asian elderly and mental health', *International Journal of Geriatric Psychiatry*, 12, p.973-977.

Sly, F. (1995) 'Ethnic groups and the labour market: analyses from the Spring 1994 Labour Force Survey', *Employment Gazette,* June, p.251-262.

Sly, F. (1996) 'Ethnic minority participation in the labour market: trends from the Labour Force Survey 1984-1995', *Labour Market Trends,* June, p.259-270.

Stewart, O. (1996) 'Yes, we mean black disabled people too', in W. Ahmad and K. Atkin (eds.), *Race and Community Care*, Buckingham: Open University Press.

Walker, R. and Ahmad W. (1994) 'Windows of opportunity in rotting frames: care providers' perspectives on community care and black communities', *Critical Social Policy*, 40, p.46-49.

Watters, C. (1996) 'Representations and realities: black people, community care and mental illness', in W. Ahmad and K. Atkin (eds.), *Race and Community Care*, Buckingham: Open University Press.

Williams, J. (1990) 'Elders from black and minority ethnic communities', in I. Sinclair, R. Parker, D. Leat, J. Williams (eds.) *The Kaleidoscope of Care: A review of research on welfare provision for elderly people,* London: HMSO, p.107-134.

Chapter 6

Older people

Jo Moriarty

Introduction

Reviewing the impact that the National Health Service and Community Care Act 1990 has had upon older people raises contradictions and tensions. From what age does one become an older person? Under what circumstances, if at all, can one make generalised comments about such a diverse group? How does one achieve a fair balance between outlining the position of the majority of older people who do not receive any community care services, at the same time as describing that of the far smaller group who use multiple services?

This brief overview attempts to consider some of these issues. First, it will outline some of the demographic evidence on the older population in the UK. Next, it will discuss some of the assumptions underpinning the way that older people are presented as consumers of community care. These ideas will be expanded in separate sections on the proportion of older people using different types of community services and the position of older carers. Finally, the overview will examine the evidence on whether older people are disadvantaged in comparison with other service users.

It is not always simple to distinguish between factors that directly relate to the implementation of the National Health Service and Community Care Act 1990 and its associated policy guidance and those that perpetuated pre-existing community care provision for older people. For example, while shifting resources from a more widespread home *help* service to a targetted home *care* service was advocated in *Caring for People* (p.26), the practice was already operational in a number of local authorities. In the same way, we need to question how stereotyped assumptions about older people may operate not only within the narrow confines of the Act but in the wider context of how resources for community care are allocated.

The older population in the UK

Decreases in infant mortality, changes in the fertility rate and increases in life expectancy have all contributed to altering the age structure of the population. Between 1961 and 1996, the overall number of people aged 65 and over rose by nearly half to 9.3 million. By 2008, it is projected that the number of people over retirement age could exceed the number of those aged under 16 for the first time. In policy terms, greatest interest has centred upon the rise in the number of people aged 85 and over. There has been a steady increase in the numbers of people in this age group, from 346,000 in 1961 to 1,067,000 in 1996. However, population projections suggest that proportionally this increase has already peaked. Between 2001 and 2021, it is estimated that the numbers of people aged 85 and over will increase from 1,163,000 to 1,459,000. By comparison, far steeper rises occurred in the 1970s and 1980s when the number of people aged 85 and over rose from 485,000 in 1971 to 896,000 in 1991. More recent work has shown that large increases in the numbers of very old people will not occur until well into the twenty-first century.

Overall population figures conceal variations. For all ages death rates are greater for men than for women, meaning that women's life expectancy is longer. Age structure varies between ethnic groups. Three per cent of people from Pakistani and Bangladeshi ethnic groups are aged 65 and over. This rises to 5% among Indians. Eight per cent of black Caribbeans are aged 65 and over, a figure which proportionally comes closest to that of the white population, of whom 16% are in this age group. In fact, the largest percentage growth in the black population has been of people aged 65 and over. In terms of this group, for the most part women do not outnumber men, as they do for the white communities. There is extensive evidence that morbidity and mortality rates vary between social classes, with people from lower social classes being disadvantaged on both counts. There are some indications that older people from minority ethnic groups may be in poorer health.

Challenging stereotypes

Slogans coined in the 1970s and 1980s to describe the changes in the age structure of the population, such as 'demographic time bomb', reflected alarmist attitudes towards the increase in the number of older citizens:

> 'The negative orientation to old age still emerges... The literature is dominated by accounts of poverty and dependence... The research problem is defined in terms of need; the data base is the needy. The silent majority of elderly people who are independent and self-supporting are not featured, are not of interest, and, if the literature is taken to reflect reality, hardly exist.'

> (Jerrome, 1992 p.3-4)

Because the likelihood of acute and long term illness increases with age, the growth in the numbers of older people led to fears about an escalating demand for services. Certainly, advancing age is associated with the use of both health and social services, but age alone is not as powerful a predictor of service use as other factors, such as the level of disability. The General Household Survey (GHS) gives us information on community service receipt from a sample of 3,501 people aged 65 and over. Well over half the respondents reported a longstanding illness, disability or infirmity. The increased need for help with self care was particularly striking in the over 80s. For instance, while only 4% of 65-69 year olds reported that they needed help taking a bath or shower, 14% of 80-84 year olds did. Domestic tasks generally caused people more problems than self care.

This has important implications when we consider the impact of the shift in the focus of home care services later. Eight per cent had received help from a local authority home care worker and 7% had used private help.

Allowing for slight changes in question wording, between 1991 and 1994 there would appear to have been no change in the number of people receiving help from their local authority but an increase in the number using private help. There was a strong relationship between a need for assistance with self care, particularly in bathing or moving about the house. Consistent with the pre-1993 picture, receipt of domiciliary services was much higher among people living alone. Negative assumptions about the consequences of an ageing population rarely seem to acknowledge the complexities of the debate about whether healthier conditions throughout the life course will lead to morbidity being compressed or expanded, or whether the process will differ between different sub-groups of the population. Another important factor helping to maintain negative images of ageing has been the way in which portrayals of older people as consumers of community care services have often failed to show their role as *providers.* In particular, older people have been shown to contribute over a third of the total volume of unpaid non-professional care received by older people. In the same way, the role of grandparents in supporting their families is increasingly recognised.

There have been attempts to counterbalance these stereotypes. The idea of the Third Age, with its emphasis on opportunities for achieving personal fulfilment, was developed in order to construct a more positive image of ageing. It is increasingly recognised that the word 'older people' is conceptually imprecise, encompassing as it may definitions of age that are chronologically or physiologically based with those that are structural (for example, people who have reached the state retirement age). The adoption of a life course approach, which emphasises the interlinkage between phases in life rather than seeing each one in isolation:

> 'eschews a static view of old age in isolation, providing a dynamic framework which focuses on change and continuity... Older people are not a homogeneous group. A span of thirty years separates recently retired elderly people from those in their nineties.'

(Arber and Evandrou, 1993 p.10)

Men and women follow different life-course paths leading to variations in economic well being and family resources throughout later life. Thus, when considering the position of older people, the impact of gender must also be taken into account.

Research on community care services for older people completed since 1993

Apart from the General Household Survey, studies based upon data collected post April 1993 tend to be both limited in number and scale.

However, the Evaluation of Community Care for Elderly People (ECCEP) study is currently being undertaken by the Personal Social Service Research Unit (PSSRU) in ten local authorities. In comparison with data from an earlier study, results suggest that services were benefiting a wider range of people and more likely to produce outcomes valued by users (such as extending length of stay in the community) and carers (such as reducing carer stress).

Debates over targeting

Set against the positive data suggesting improved relationships between needs and service provision for the fewer older people needing most care, disquiet has been expressed about what happens to the greater number of older people needing less assistance. It has been suggested that the provision of 'low level' services, such as help with housework, laundry, gardening and repairs, enhances older people's quality of life and helps them maintain their independence. In the same way, while the continuing focus of domiciliary services upon older people living alone is seen as reducing risk, it does not take account of the very high levels of disability found in two or more person households. However, the latter could not be helped simply by redeploying services from the former, as high rates of long term illness exist among those living alone.

Balancing residential care and community services

It is not always recognised that the proportion of the older population living in residential care settings has remained at a consistently low level throughout the last one hundred years. Part of the importance of using good information on the age structure of the older population as the basis for making policy decisions on the range of services to be provided and how they are to be funded stems from the differences in rates of entry to residential care between different age groups. Thus, in 1991 only 1% of 65-69 year olds were in residential care. The equivalent figure for those aged 85 and over was 24%. Expressed another way, at the age of 30 men have a one in five chance and women a one in three chance of needing residential care before they die.

Concern has been expressed about the way in which rates of entry to residential care vary between different social services departments. We have, however, to consider the impact of *local* differences in the age structure of the population served by each authority. These are so large that even if national patterns of placement in residential care were to be applied, local rates of placement would still vary. Variations in the eligibility criteria imposed by local authorities and the levels and types of community care services available locally may also influence the number of people in residential care. There is strong evidence that one of the effects of the National Health Service and Community Care Act 1990 has been to reduce the number of older people admitted to residential care. One estimate is that 60,000 fewer people are in residential care than would have been the case had the changes not taken place. However, in terms of the balance between residential care services and community provision, so called perverse incentives still exist in favour of residential care. Current funding arrangements mean that the length of stay and turnover of residents have important financial and administrative implications for local authorities. As the number of local authority supported residents increases, there are indications that budgets for other community care services are being 'squeezed'. For instance in 1996 almost half the local authorities cut the hours of home care that they provided. The rate of 49 older people in residential care per 1,000 people aged 65 and over compares with 34 people per 1,000 receiving meals and 20 local authority purchased day care places per 1,000.

Older carers

There is now an established literature identifying the number of older people who themselves care for another person. However, the needs of older carers are not always recognised. While they tend to care for shorter periods, it is more likely to involve giving intimate personal care and carrying out heavy nursing tasks. Older carers tend to be caring for their spouse and this involves different dynamics from those, for instance, in helping a neighbour. Services that are seen as indirectly supporting carers, such as short stays or day care, tend to be more readily used by daughters. There is evidence that many spouse carers are reluctant to arrange short stay care in homes or hospitals and would prefer home based respite that would, for instance, enable them to catch up on their sleep or do gardening uninterrupted. Because older carers are more likely to have health problems of their own, they are especially likely to value assistance with physically demanding tasks such as housework. Thus a service strategy aimed at supporting older carers might involve offering more help with domestic chores and more frequent home based breaks instead of a short stay lasting a fortnight.

As carers' issues have become better recognised, the importance of engaging with and supporting carers has become more accepted. However, concern has been expressed that where mechanisms for recording and acting on unmet need are not effective, carers become very dependent upon collective representation through carer consultations as a way of influencing service provision. This may lead to under-representation of some groups of carers, particularly those from minority ethnic groups. Although the policy guidance issued in conjunction with the Carers (Recognition and Services) Act 1995 emphasised the role of the NHS in supporting carers, a survey of members of the Carers National Association suggested that few carers had been given information or training, for instance in lifting techniques, by NHS staff.

Are older users disadvantaged?

For older people, one of the most important issues in evaluating the impact of the National Health Service and Community Care Act 1990 is the way in which they continue to be disadvantaged in comparison with other groups. This can be demonstrated in the following ways:

- The original Direct Payments Act applied an upper age limit, although the White Paper *Modernising Social Services* has promised that the legislation will be amended.

- It seems that many authorities operate lower limits on community care packages for older adults than younger users. Older people are the largest *user* group and so tighter eligibility policies designed to restrict services are likely to affect them most. Proportionally more of the budget for younger adults (18-64) is spent on day and domiciliary services than on long term care. By contrast, most of the budget for older people is being spent on long term care. This may be partly an effect of encouraging older people to seek residential or nursing care once their care package costs rise above a certain level.

- It has been suggested that society's attitudes to older people's rights lags far behind that towards other groups. It is still comparatively rare to find evidence of older people being involved in decisions about service planning, although positive developments for the future include the establishment of a national Older People's Advocacy Alliance and the growth of senior citizens forums. At the same time, further efforts need to be made to ensure that the voices of less vocal older people, such as the housebound or from minority ethnic groups, are heard.

Discussion

This last section aims to show that progress since April 1993 in terms of delivering services to older people has not been consistent. On the one hand, it has been suggested that specialist disability teams are more likely to offer comprehensive assessments and to recognise people's rights to an assessment than generic or older people's teams. On the other, it is now more frequent to find qualified staff undertaking older people's assessments than in the past. In the same way, two of the few studies that have been able to directly compare pre and post April 1993 provision have suggested that older people living at home receive *more* services than did people with similar levels of disability before the Act, both in England and in Scotland. Set against this, we must consider the viewpoint of those who argue that policies of intensive service targeting have increased inequities and fail to promote independence. One of the key issues for the future is how to distinguish better between community care services that are best delivered in an intensive way to a highly targeted group of people and those universalist services, such as a short term care attendant scheme for people discharged from hospital, whose cost effectiveness would have been reduced had it only been available to a restricted group.

The second is a requirement for a broader perspective towards the effects of different Government departments' policies upon older people. For instance, as more social services departments charge nearer the full economic cost of domiciliary services and tighten their eligibility criteria, the question of older people's incomes becomes more and more important. While many older people are prepared to buy in the help they want, the market for domestic help varies throughout the country. Older people living in areas where there is a considerable demand for housework or gardening may find that the 'going rate' is more than they can afford. We also have to consider the impact of the widening gap in pensioner incomes. In 1994/95, the poorest 20% of pensioner couples had a weekly net income of £71.40 per week, an increase in real terms of 28% since 1979. By comparison, at £273 the income of the richest 20% had increased by 61%. A positive feature of the Better Government for Older People initiative is that it seeks to deal with the questions that affect older people in an integrated way.

Finally, there is a need to negotiate between the objectives of policy makers, service planners and professionals and the preferences of older people themselves. As an example, while older people see having a clean and tidy home as a desirable and important outcome, the provision of cleaning services by social services departments has been reduced substantially. Similarly, while users value continuity in home care staff and flexibility in what they are prepared to do, this may conflict with practices such as spot purchasing and overly precise contract specifications. It is noticeable that the failure to provide domestic support is at odds with needs identified through central Government supported research, research completed prior to the reforms and the preferences of older people themselves. It is essential that the voice of older people themselves should play a stronger part in determining how community care services should develop in the future and that there should be greater recognition of how life experiences, social class, age, gender, culture and ethnicity, and social support throughout the life course are likely to contribute to a diversity of needs and aspirations.

The sources on which this section draws are listed at the end of Chapter 7.

Chapter 7

Chapter 7

Older people with dementia and their carers

Jo Moriarty

Older people with dementia and their carers were a prime target for the new arrangements for community care. Prior to the implementation of the NHS and Community Care Act 1990, there was an established literature on older people with dementia and their carers. It suggested that people with dementia were at increased risk of entry to residential care; while an inability to carry out activities of daily living (ADLs) independently as a result of dementia meant that they were also major users of home care and day care services; there were still high levels of unmet need; 'standard' community services were not always flexible and able to cater for the specific needs of people with dementia and their carers; and carers of people with dementia were at greater risk of poor psychological health than other carers.

The six key objectives outlined in *Caring for People* highlighted the inherent conflicts in the way that the projected legislation would affect people with dementia. On the one hand, they might stand to benefit from the development of day, domiciliary, and respite services and an explicit aim to improve support for carers. On the other, would targeting services upon those in greatest need disadvantage people with moderate or severe dementia living in the community who, because they are more likely to be living with a carer, might be perceived as being at less 'risk' than people living alone? Most importantly of all, how would the needs of people whose condition was likely to have affected their ability to express preferences and make choices be served under a new expressly consumerist philosophy? In their review of the first year of the Act, the Association of Directors of Social Services (ADSS) reported that the service users who gave departments the greatest difficulty and cause for concern were – for all types of authority – elderly people suffering from mental infirmity or dementia and especially those presenting challenging behaviour (1994 p.4). The report appeared to reflect an increasing awareness of the need to take account of people with dementia, both in the planning and delivery of community care services.

What do we know about how this was operating in practice? One of the chief difficulties in answering this question is that no research designed to compare directly the pre and post April 1993 situation was funded. The Social Services Inspectorate have conducted two inspections, one on assessment, the other on services for people living at home. However, so far, there is only limited published information specifically looking at services for people with dementia that is based on data collected post April 1993 and in this context, the Department of Health funded research looking at people with dementia assessed by their local social services department undertaken by NISW (Moriarty and Webb, 1998) is currently one of the main sources. The study involved studying the records of 14 social work teams and following up a sample of 141 people with dementia. Separate interviews took place with assessors, proxy informants such as staff working in residential homes, carers and people with dementia. The latter three groups were re-interviewed approximately 11 months later.

The data suggested some positive findings. Almost 90% of people were assessed within a month of referral and arrangements seemed to have been made to allow carers to be present, and to allow carers, and to a slightly lesser extent, the older people with dementia, to express their viewpoints. Carers appeared to be receiving greater assistance with the personal care of the person with dementia from services than in earlier research. The receipt of home care and day care were statistically significantly associated with people remaining at home. Costings work completed by PSSRU showed that people were being offered community care packages at costs equivalent to, or higher than, places in long term care. However, at the same time, very little specialist home care was available, although this is a service regularly positively evaluated by carers and enables people with dementia to have a choice between that and day care.

Levels of community service receipt were lower than in a specialist care management scheme completed shortly before the Act but higher than in community samples using post April 1993 data. Most carers had been caring for some time before being referred. Debates about the merits of early intervention and preventative work will remain academic if people continue to be unaware of what is provided and how to access it.

Issues for the future

Two issues emerge from this brief review. First, it is clear that the marketplace approach to community care, where service users are treated as consumers, able to demand service and to argue for improvements, is particularly inappropriate in the case of older people with dementia. Our view is that while there is a sense of raised expectations and perhaps more readiness amongst carers to criticise services, in themselves these pressures are insufficient to raise standards or to change services fundamentally. Secondly, there is little evidence that the new arrangements for community care have created variety in the services available to older people with dementia and to their carers. The services remain, perhaps appropriately, focused on home care and day care, with a majority using these two main services only. Certainly, there is the traditional need to ensure users are well informed about these services, but the evidence suggests, and market analysts such as Laing and Buisson confirm, that a multiplicity of small providers is not a current or future reality. In addition, home care services remain firmly fixed on the personal care needs of older people with dementia, although this group of people also have social care needs.

The two chapters above draw on the following sources:

Arber, S. and Evandrou, M. (1993) 'Mapping the territory: ageing, independence and the life course', in S. Arber and M. Evandrou (eds.) *Ageing, Independence and the Life Course*, London: Jessica Kingsley.

Arber, S. and Ginn, J. (1990) 'The meaning of informal care: gender and the contribution of elderly people', *Ageing and Society,* 10, p.429-54.

Arber, S. and Ginn, J. (1991) *Gender and Later Life: A Sociological Analysis of Resources and Constraints*, London: Sage Publications.

Arber, S. and Ginn, J. (1993) 'Class, caring and the life course', in A. Arber and M. Evandrou (eds.) *Ageing, Independence and the Life Course*, London: Jessica Kingsley.

Association of Directors of Social Services (1994) *Towards Community Care: ADSS review of the first year*, London: ADSS.

Audit Commission (1997) *The Coming of Age: Improving care services for older people*, London: Audit Commission.

Barton, A., Coles, O., Stone, M. and Dodds, M. (1990) 'Home help and home care for the frail elderly: face to face in Darlington', *Research, Policy and Planning,* 8, 1, p.7-13.

Bennett, N., Jarvis, L., Rowlands, O., Singleton, N. and Hasleden, L. (1996) *Living in Britain: Results from the 1994 General Household Survey*, London: HMSO.

Boniface, D. and Denham, M. (1997) 'Factors influencing the use of community health and social services by those aged 65 and over', *Health and Social Care in the Community,* 5, 1, p.48-54.

Bowling, A., Farquar, M. and Grundy, E. (1993) 'Who are the consistently high users of health and social services? A follow up study two and a half years later of people aged 85 plus at baseline', *Health and Social Care in the Community,* 1, p.277-87.

Buck, D., Gregson, B., Bamford, C., McNamee, P., Farrow, G., Bond, J. and Wright, K. (1997) 'Psychological distress among informal supporters of frail older people at home and in institutions', *International Journal of Geriatric Psychiatry*, 12, p.737-744.

Burholt, V., Wenger, G. and Scott, A. (1997) 'Dementia, disability and contact with formal services: a comparison of dementia sufferers and non-sufferers in rural and urban settings', *Health and Social Care in the Community*, 5, 6, p.384-397.

Butt, J. and Mirza, K. (1996) *Social Care and Black Communities*, London: HMSO.

Challis, D., Darton, R., Johnson, L., Stone, M. and Traske, K. (1995) *Care Management and Health Care of Older People: The Darlington community care project*, Aldershot: Arena.

Challis, D., von Abendorff, R., Brown, P. and Chesterman, J. (1997) 'Care management and dementia: an evaluation of the Lewisham intensive case management scheme', in S. Hunter (ed.) *Dementia: Challenges and new directions*, London: Jessica Kingsley, p.139-164.

Clark, H., Dyer, S. and Horwood, J. (1998) *'That Bit of Help': The high value of low level preventative services for older people*, Bristol: Policy Press.

Cullen, M., Blizard, R., Livingston, G., and Mann, A. (1993) 'The Gospel Oak project 1987-1990: provision and use of community services', *Health Trends,* 25, p.142-6.

Darton, R. (1994) 'Length of stay of residents and patients in residential and nursing homes for elderly people', *Research, Policy and Planning,* 12, 3, p.18-24.

Davis, A., Ellis, K. and Rummery, K. (1998) *Access to Assessment: Perspectives of practitioners, disabled people and carers*, York: Joseph Rowntree Foundation.

Department of Social Security (1997) *Social Security Statistics 1997*, London: The Stationery Office.

Dunning, A. (1998) 'Better government, engagement and prevention', *Prevention Works*, 5, p.7.

ECCEP Team (1998) *ECCEP Bulletin*, Canterbury: Personal Social Services Research Unit.

Edwards, P. and Kenny, D. (1997) *Community Care Trends 1997,* London: Local Government Management Board.

Fisher, M. (1990) 'Care management and social work: clients with dementia', *Practice,* 4, 4, p.229-241.

Ginn, J., Arber, S. and Cooper, H. (1997) *Researching Older People's Health Needs and Health Promotion Issues*, London: Health Education Authority.

Glaser, K., Murphy, M. and Grundy, E. (1997) 'Limiting long term illness and household structure among people aged 45 and over, Great Britain 1991', *Ageing and Society,* 17, 1 p.3-19.

Harding, T. (1997) *A Life Worth Living: The independence and inclusion of older people*, London: Help the Aged.

Henwood, M. (1998) *Ignored and Invisible? Carers' experiences of the NHS*, London: Carers National Association.

Henwood, M., Lewis, H. and Waddington, E. (1998) *Listening to Users of Domiciliary Care Services: Developing and monitoring quality standards*, Leeds: Nuffield Institute for Health.

Jerrome, D. (1992) *Good Company: An anthropological study of old people in groups*, Edinburgh: Edinburgh University Press.

Johnson, P. and Falkingham, J. (1992) *Ageing and Economic Welfare*, London: Sage Publications.

Joseph Rowntree Foundation Inquiry (1996) *Meeting the Costs of Continuing Care*, York: Joseph Rowntree Foundation.

Laing, W. and Saper, P. (1998) *Objective 4: To promote the development of a flourishing independent sector alongside good quality public services* paper presented to seminar for the Royal Commission on Long Term Care, Leeds, October.

Laslett, P. (1989) *A Fresh Map of Life: The emergence of the third age*, London: Weidenfield and Nicholson.

Levin, E., Sinclair, I. and Gorbach, P. (1989) *Families, Services and Confusion in Old Age,* Aldershot: Avebury.

Levin, E., Moriarty, J. and Gorbach, P. (1994) *Better for the Break*, London: HMSO.

Levin, E. and Webb, S. (1997) *Social Work and Community Care: Changing roles and tasks*, London: National Institute for Social Work.

Lewis, J. and Glennerster, H. (1996) *Implementing the New Community Care*, Buckingham: Open University Press.

Livingston, G., Manela, M. and Katona, C. (1997) 'Cost of community care for older people', *British Journal of Psychiatry,* 171, p.56-69.

Livingston, G., Thomas, A., Graham, N., Blizard, B. and Mann, A. (1990) 'The Gospel Oak Project: the use of health and social services by dependent elderly people in the community', *Health Trends*, 22, p.70-73.

McMullin, J. (1995) 'Theorising age and gender relations', in S. Arber and J. Ginn (eds.) *Connecting Gender and Ageing*, Buckingham: Open University Press. p.30-41.

Melzer, D., Ely, M. and Brayne, C. (1997) 'Local population differences and the needs of people with cognitive impairment', *International Journal of Geriatric Psychiatry,* 12, p.883-7.

Moriarty, J. and Webb, S. (1998) *Part of their Lives: An evaluation of community care for older people with dementia*, London: NISW Research Unit.

O'Connor, D., Pollitt, P., Hyde, J., Fellows, J., Miller, N., Brook, C., Reiss, B. and Roth, M. (1989) 'The prevalence of dementia as measured by the Cambridge Mental Disorders of the Elderly Examination', *Acta Psychiatrica Scandanavia*, 79, p.190-198.

Office for National Statistics (1998a) *Annual Abstract of Statistics*, London: The Stationery Office.

Office for National Statistics (1998b) *Social Trends 28*, London: The Stationery Office.

Olsen, R., Parker, G. and Drewett, A. (1997) 'Carers and the missing link: changing professional attitudes', *Health and Social Care in the Community,* 5, 2, p.116-23.

Opit, L. and Pahl, J. (1993) 'Institutional care for elderly people: can we predict admissions?', *Research, Policy and Planning,* 10, 2, p.2-5.

Parker, G. and Lawton, D. (1994) *Different Types of Care, Different Types of Carer: Evidence from the General Household Survey*, London: HMSO.

Petch, A., Cheetham, J., Fuller, R., MacDonald, C., Myers, F., with Hallam, A. and Knapp, M. (1996) *Delivering Community Care: Initial implementation of care management in Scotland*, Edinburgh: The Stationery Office.

Philp, I., McKee, K., Meldrum, P., Ballinger, B., Gilhooly, M., Gordon, D., Mutch, W. and Whittick, J. (1995) 'Community care for demented and non-demented elderly people: a comparison study of financial burden, service use and unmet needs in family supporters', *British Medical Journal,* 310, p.1503-06.

Qureshi, H., Patmore, C., Nicholas, E. and Bamford, C. (1998) *Overview: Outcomes of social care for older people and carers*, Outcomes in Community Care Practice No. 5, York: Social Policy Research Unit.

Riorden, J. and Bennett, A. (1998) 'An evaluation of an augmented domiciliary service to older people with dementia and their carers', *Aging and Mental Health,* 2, 2, p.137-143.

Schneider, J., Kavanagh, S., Knapp, M., Beecham, J. and Netten, A. (1993) 'Elderly people with advanced cognitive impairment in England: resource use and costs', *Age and Ageing,* 13, p.27-50.

Secretary of State (1989) *Caring for People: Community Care in the Next Decade and Beyond*, Cm. 849, London: HMSO.

Townsend, J., Piper, M., Frank, A., Dyer, S., North, W. and Meade, T. (1988) 'Reduction in hospital readmission stay of elderly patients by a community based hospital discharge scheme: a randomized control trial', *British Medical Journal,* 297, p.544-7.

Twigg, J., Atkin, K. and Perring, C. (1990) *Carers and Services: A review of research*, London: HMSO.

Wenger, G. (1990) 'Elderly carers: the need for appropriate intervention', *Ageing and Society,* 10, p.197-219.

Wilson, G. (1994) 'Assembling their own care packages: payments for care by men and women in advanced old age', *Health and Social Care in the Community* 2, 5, p.283-91.

Chapter 8

People with learning difficulties

Don Brand

Policy background

The NHS and Community Care Act 1990 did not change the broad shape
and direction of policy and provision for people with learning disabilities.
This had been set in the 1971 White Paper *Better Services for the Mentally
Handicapped* and remained on a fairly steady course, albeit unevenly
implemented and under-resourced, through the 1970s and 1980s. Its
objectives were to reduce the population of the long stay learning disability
hospitals (the subject of a number of major abuse enquiries between 1969
and 1977) and improve conditions for those remaining; transfer the 'abler
residents' to community care; increase the volume of community-based
residential and day services to provide alternatives to hospital admission;
and enhance joint working between health and social services.

Government measures to implement the policy included a local authority
hostel and day centre building programme in the early 1970s; the
influential Jay Committee report on staffing and training; developments in
joint finance arrangements during the 1970s, to allow transfer of NHS
resources (sometimes in the form of 'dowry payments' attached to
individual hospital residents) to fund more appropriate social services
provision; and a major DHSS-sponsored programme of community care
demonstration projects in the mid 1980s, evaluated by PSSRU, to test new
ways of resettling long stay hospital residents in smaller scale
community-based placements. In Wales, central Government and local
authorities collaborated in developing and implementing the All Wales
Strategy for learning disability services.

The development of community care was also influenced, and arguably
distorted, by the increasing availability through the 1980s of social security
benefit funding for individual placements in registered private residential
homes, allocated on demand with a means test but without an assessment
of care needs. Similarly, rising levels of housing benefit, and access to
capital through the Housing Corporation, encouraged an increase in
supported housing schemes run by housing associations for various
groups with special needs, including people with learning disabilities.

Value base for service development

Alongside these policy-led developments, learning disability services were
strongly influenced by the promotion of a distinctive value base which
stressed de-institutionalisation, 'normalisation' and the benefits of 'ordinary
living' for people with disabilities. Service models reflecting these values,

promulgated since the 1970s by a range of research and development institutes, have challenged traditional institutional styles of provision. O'Brien's 'five accomplishments' have become a yardstick for the effectiveness of flexible, individualised support in the community for people with learning disabilities. Quality standards, used for example by the Social Services Inspectorate in inspecting services, have incorporated principles of individuality, privacy, dignity and choice. Increasingly, user and self advocacy groups have argued for greater independence and access to ordinary living, and asserted their claim to be consulted in their own right rather than have parents and professionals speak for them.

Intentions of the 1990 Act

The aim of the 1990 Act was to create an explicit planning, priority setting, resource allocation and quality assurance framework to support the development and management of community care services and deliver improved value for money. The *Caring for People* White Paper had identified the priorities: enabling people to be maintained independently in their own homes where possible; providing better support for carers; promoting high quality public services within a mixed economy of provision; allocating services on the basis of assessed need, and targeting those in greatest need; tailoring services to individual requirements; and giving users and their families a stronger voice through formal inspection and complaints procedures.

The legislation and accompanying policy guidance provided the administrative means to these ends: community care plans, assessment and care management processes, inspection units independent of the line management of local authority services, complaints procedures, and the phased transfer of responsibilities and resources from social security to local authorities. Additional guidance and further legislation sought to refine the framework, with the direction on choice of residential home; the Carers Act entitling carers to ask for their own needs to be separately assessed; and the direct payments provision, by which authorities can make payments to users to secure their own care and employ staff directly to meet their assessed needs.

Impact on people with learning disabilities

On the face of it, the policy aims of the 1990 Act were broadly consistent with the previous direction of policy and practice in services for people with learning disabilities. Individual programme planning (IPP), an assessment format widely used with learning disabled people, was designed to promote independence and self determination, and enable them to remain in or return to the community with the support of flexible services tailored to their individual needs. It was quite compatible with the guidance on assessment and care management.

Perhaps significantly, guidance circulars on local authority and health authority roles and responsibilities in services for people with learning disabilities, issued by the Department of Health in 1992, were notably non-prescriptive about the direction of service development. Beyond outlining the areas of social care for which local authorities had responsibility, and encouraging access for people with learning disabilities to mainstream health, education, employment and leisure services, the circulars gave little indication of any Government preference for particular models of service or methods of promoting the greater integration in the community of people with learning disabilities. They appeared to assume the new community care arrangements would produce their own momentum.

Improvements in community care

The indications are that existing trends towards somewhat less institutional forms of service have continued within the new framework. More people with learning disabilities are living in ordinary houses in the community, generally on a shared basis with two or three others, or sometimes more. Support schemes have been developed for those in further education, and there are more learning programmes adapted to their needs, often with effective use of IT developments. There is increased use of individual activity programmes using a mixture of day centre, educational and community facilities, as an alternative to daily attendance at a centre. There is better access to a wider range of mainstream leisure activities and holiday locations.

There has been some increase in opportunities for employment, both in supported placements with existing employers, and in the development of social firms and work projects in the retail and service sectors, often with some support from European funding. Service users and their families have more opportunity to be involved in plans for their own care and support, to be consulted on service developments and participate in quality monitoring and inspection. A major national voluntary organisation, Mencap, is introducing a new general assembly, one third of whose members will be people with learning disabilities, with real power in all aspects of Mencap's decision making. More effort is made to provide information in appropriate formats for people with learning disabilities. Community care plans publish information on current and planned provision in health and social care.

Slow and uneven implementation

These trends are by no means uniform or consistent, however. There are plenty of old style larger scale hostels and social education centres continuing to provide segregated group care and day activities. Indeed, significant numbers of people are still living in long stay hospitals. Families of people with learning disabilities are still faced with a drastic change in levels and quality of support and opportunities when their young people leave the education system and transfer to community care services. As with other client groups, assessment of needs, and service planning through care management, can often result in individual users being fitted into the limited range of facilities available in the locality, rather than receiving a package of support tailored to their particular needs and aspirations. Revelations of severe and long standing abuse of residents at the Longcare homes in Buckinghamshire have also raised questions about the effectiveness of registration and inspection in enforcing standards in residential care.

Negative consequences

In some respects, the impact of the new arrangements may also have been to the disadvantage of some people with learning disabilities. The effect of targeting services on those in greatest need, in a context of budget constraints, has been to raise eligibility levels for service, and in some cases restrict or remove support for those with lower levels of disability. In some areas, pressure on local authority budgets has led to the introduction of new charges to users for travel to and attendance at day facilities.

A study by Values into Action of resettlement schemes in nine areas found some NHS learning difficulties trusts were continuing to dominate service planning and provision, in some cases resisting the policy of hospital closure and maintaining residents' needs were too difficult to be met in the community. It also found health authority and social services department commissioners often lacked knowledge of the kinds of services users wanted, and relied for advice on the service providers. Despite guidance circulars encouraging local negotiation and agreement, disputes remain about the respective responsibilities of the NHS and social services for the continuing care and support of people with complex and multiple disabilities, including those whose learning disabilities are combined with severe physical disabilities, mental health problems or challenging behaviour.

Expectations outpacing policy

There is also a good deal of evidence that the newer forms of service provision are failing to keep pace with the developing needs and expectations of people with learning disabilities. There are shortfalls in quantity and quality. Estimates of need for suitable housing and employment opportunities are far in excess of the volume of provision so far available. Shared accommodation in ordinary houses may be better than life on the hospital ward, but for people who now want to move on to independent accommodation (often to get away from intrusion by other residents or support staff), the opportunities are very few. Innovative schemes like the living support networks established by the Keyring agency and the housing with support models described by Simons (1995) have had to overcome the obstacles of professional preconceptions and a tendency by purchasers to opt for institutionalised, not individualised, solutions.

'Life has got better. I've got a house, got a room, no interference. More freedom. The best day of my life was leaving Leybourne [long-stay hospital]. I went to live in Beckwood Hill. I lived there with Alice. I'd like to know if she's still alive, because she was my friend. Gerry [staff] helped me in Beckwood Hill. He is one of the best friends I ever had. I used to walk down to Safeways to get my shopping. I could walk better then.

I went to live in Horne Road, which was all right, but I didn't see anyone. Since I've lived at Alderton Way, I have enjoyed going shopping, going to the pictures, theatre, buying teddies.

The best place I lived was Beckwood Hill – I wish I was back there. I like living on my own better – more freedom. I have had some nice people work with me over the years, and I miss them. It's a better life now altogether.'

Jean, a service user with MCCH, Kent, *MCCH Newsletter*, Spring 1998

The growth of supported housing schemes has been an important element in expanding community care, but such schemes often lack the flexibility to provide on-going support when people move to alternative accommodation, or to allow people to stay in familiar accommodation if they no longer need support. Many authorities have been slow to implement the direct payments legislation in respect of people with physical disabilities, and its possible benefits in increased independence for those with learning disabilities have yet to be fully explored. Values into Action has produced a useful guide, *Funding Freedom*, on how direct payments can be used flexibly and with safeguards for the benefit of people with learning disabilities.

Scope to participate in 'real work', and receive proper wages rather than 'pocket money', has been restricted for many by rigidities in the benefits system. With very limited incomes, people with learning disabilities also miss out on opportunities to participate in mainstream entertainment, sporting and leisure activities, and can find themselves still relatively isolated and excluded. At the same time, the reluctance of services and staff (and sometimes families) to address issues of sexuality for people with learning disabilities has been a factor in restricting their access to an ordinary social life and satisfying sexual relationships.

'If it wasn't for Kwikbite [supported employment scheme], I don't know what I'd do all day, really. Coming here makes me get up in the mornings and I look forward to my whole day. Before I was working here I just used to sit about and watch telly...'

> 'Kwikbite isn't like other jobs I've had. It's more like a real job. I get paid a proper wage as well, so I can save up and buy my own things.'
>
> Learning disabled service users, interviewed for an evaluation of the employment scheme by the Tizard Centre, Kent University (Mason and Hughes, 1998)

Conclusions

The community care framework put in place by the 1990 Act has created opportunities for more individualised support, access to a wider range of community services, and greater participation in service planning and review for people with learning disabilities. It has not, however, produced the drive to secure these outcomes for the majority of users. Some have been disadvantaged by the direct or unintended effects of the changes, and many continue to experience the effects of poverty, isolation and restricted involvement in community life. Central Government has not been sufficiently active in setting the direction for policy implementation; and local authorities have too often applied a narrow interpretation of their community care lead role, focussing on assessment, care management and purchasing tasks, rather than using a commissioning approach to reshape services to meet users' rising expectations and promote better access to housing, education, training and employment.

This section draws on the following sources:

Beyer, S. and Kilsby, M. (1996) 'Future of employment for people with learning disabilities', *British Journal of Learning Disability,* 24, p.134.

Burgner, T. (1998) *Independent Longcare Inquiry,* Buckingham: Buckinghamshire County Council.

Collins, J. (1993) *The Resettlement Game: Continuing institutional care for people with learning difficulties,* London: Values into Action.

Dee, S. (1998) 'Changing educational opportunities for people with learning difficulties following the Tomlinson Report', *Tizard Learning Disability Review,* 3, 3, p.16.

DHSS (1976) *Joint Care Planning: Health and local authorities,* LAC 76(6), London: DHSS.

Department of Health (1998) *Community Care: An agenda for action* (The Griffiths Report), London: HMSO.

Department of Health (1989) *Caring for People: Community care in the next decade and beyond,* London: HMSO.

Department of Health (1991) *Implementing Caring for People: Guidance on assessment and care management,* London: Department of Health.

Department of Health (1992) *Guidance on Social Care for People with Learning Disabilities,* LAC(92)15, London: Department of Health.

Department of Health (1994) *Implementing Caring for People: 'It's our lives' – community care for people with learning disabilities,* Lancashire: BAPS, Health Publication Unit.

Department of Health (1998) *Moving into the Mainstream: SSI report on inspection of services for adults with learning disabilities,* London: Department of Health.

Holland, A. (1997) 'People living in community homes: their views', *British Journal of Learning Disability,* 25, p.68.

Holman, A. and Collins, H. (1997) *Funding Freedom: A guide to direct payments for people with learning difficulties,* London: Values into Action.

Jay Committee (1979) *Report of the Committee of Enquiry into Mental Handicap Nursing and Care,* London: HMSO.

Knapp, M. et al. (1991) *Care in the Community: Final report,* Canterbury: PSSRU.

Malhotra, S. and Mellan, B. (1996) 'Cultural and race issues in sexuality work with people with learning difficulties', *Tizard Learning Disability Review,* 1, 4.

Mason, J. and Hughes, A. (1998) *Independent Evaluation: The viability of the Kwikbite Project from a trainee perspective,* Canterbury: Tizard Centre.

Mental Health Foundation (1996) *Building Expectations: Report of committee of inquiry,* London: Mental Health Foundation.

O'Brien, J. and Lyle, C. (1987) *A Framework for Accomplishment,* Atlanta, Georgia: Responsive Systems Associates.

Rix, B. (1999) 'Learning to try', *Guardian,* 13 January.

Joseph Rowntree Foundation (1993) *Community Living for People with Learning Difficulties* (The Keyring Project), York: Joseph Rowntree Foundation.

Joseph Rowntree Foundation (1998) 'Low support options for people with learning difficulties', *JRF Findings,* 528.

Simons, K. (1995) *My Home, My Life: Innovative ideas in housing and support for people with learning difficulties,* London: Values into Action.

Simons, K. (1997) 'Residential care, or housing and support', *British Journal of Learning Disability,* 25, p.2.

Simons, K (1998) *Living Support Networks: The services provided by Keyring,* Brighton: Pavilion Publishing.

Towell, D. (ed.) (1988) *An Ordinary Life in Practice,* London: Kings Fund.

Towell, D. (1997) 'Promoting a better life for people with learning disabilities and their families: a practical agenda for the new Government', *British Journal of Learning Disability,* 25, p.90.

Watson, L. and Harker, M. (1993) *Community Care Planning: A model for housing needs assessment with reference to people with learning disabilities*, London: Institute of Housing.

Chapter 9

Rationing, charging and costs

Sue Balloch

Introduction

In implementing the NHS and Community Care Act 1990 a number of vital issues were not fully taken into account: firstly, the increasing longevity of both frail older people and younger adults with severe disabilities meant greater resources would be needed for domiciliary support to enable them to live at home; secondly, the care of people with either physical or mental health problems in the community would require special facilities and joint working between health, social services and housing agencies; thirdly, those most heavily dependent on the state, rather than on families and friends for care, were those with the lowest incomes, receiving income support and other benefits. Because of this, the implementation of the 1990 Act was both underfunded and not coherently related to the social security system. One commentator has gone so far as to claim that the NHS and Community Care Act represented an 'administrative mechanism for curtailing state expenditure on welfare and on the poorest in particular, and is an essential component of the strategy to restructure the welfare state'.

Under the Act responsibility for the funding of placements in residential care and nursing homes passed from central to local government. Previously people had entered residential and nursing care using DSS funding, with numbers and consequent expenditure rising dramatically following the Residential Homes Act 1984. Funding was transferred through the special transitional grant (STG) and this increased Government funding to social services departments by 63% between 1992/93 and 1997/98. However, this transfer took place against a 6% real decrease in spending on the personal social services through the standard spending assessment (SSA), leaving local authorities to fund more than double the number of residents they support in residential and nursing homes and provide nearly 800,000 extra home help contact hours per week than was the case in 1993. This is the context within which local authorities have become increasingly concerned about diminishing resources for community care, with changes in their assessment of their duties and obligations towards users.

The local authority associations estimated that community care would be underfunded by £135m in its first year and that this deficit was set to increase in subsequent years. One of the repercussions of inadequate funding has been the development of systems of rationing in local authorities based on increased charges and a tightening of eligibility criteria for services. For example, the London Borough of Brent, having lost £8.5 million as a result of changes to the SSA at the end of 1998, implemented cuts of £2.8 million to its social services budget, £1 million of which came from cuts in home care and £1 million from revising eligibility criteria. Around the country such rationing affects both domiciliary and residential care, even though charges for the latter are not discretionary, except in the case of respite care. It emphasises the contradiction between health services free at the point of delivery and social services for which charges may be levied.

Current inequities

Local authorities were instructed within guidance to ensure that they recouped 9% of their community care costs through charges. Almost all have done so, though the range of clawback is reported in the recent White Paper to be within 4% and 28%. Authorities in more affluent areas have obviously had greater success than those in the most deprived.

So far none of the contentious issues initially associated with charging policies and practices – inequity, exclusion and ill-founded assumptions about costs and benefits – have been resolved. Complaints have surrounded:

• lack of knowledge about the costs of care;

• raised charges accompanied by increasingly rigid eligibility criteria: these effectively screen out lower level, preventative services as well as encourage users to discontinue services;

• wide variation in policies and practices of local authorities;

• lack of information for users on charging policies.

These issues have been well covered in a major review from the National Consumer Council (1995) and three reports from the Joseph Rowntree Foundation. Following publication of these reports, JRF decided that, as carefully thought through guidelines for local authorities had already been prepared by the Association of Metropolitan Authorities and the Association of County Councils (now the Local Government Association) they would sponsor no further research or development work on charging at that time. It was for the local authorities to set their houses in order by following the guidelines available. In many cases there are no obvious signs of this happening. Moreover, the number of local authorities not charging continues to dwindle, with Manchester and Southwark introducing charging in 1997 and Newham in 1999, as well as nearly all the new unitary authorities.

Information received from members of the National Community Care Alliance in 1997 showed that charging was still contentious.

Changing rules as new eligibility criteria are imposed

There was evidence that ground rules were changing as new eligibility criteria were put in place. One authority, for example, was proposing to review criteria for those receiving home care services. This would exclude the 20% who received a service but did not have personal needs.

> '*Such a reallocation is difficult and distressing but the distress of losing a valued service which can be organised by individuals themselves in other ways has to be balanced against the Council's duty to provide personal care for highly dependent individuals who have no alternative means of getting care.*'
> Comment to a charging survey carried out among members of the National Community Care Alliance, 1997

The authority referred to the House of Lords' Judicial Review which agreed with Gloucester County Council that a local authority could take into account the availability of resources when setting eligibility criteria for services. It described its community care plan for 1996/99, in which the current eligibility criteria had been published, as 'not a static document', suggesting that not too much credence should be attached to the details such plans contain.

Another authority voiced its concern about its unintentional creation of a two tier system, in which those who had been assessed and allocated services before the introduction of new eligibility criteria were receiving more and cheaper services than those assessed afterwards.

More inroads into benefits

Some local authorities appeared to be increasing their efforts to claim payments towards the cost of home care from benefits. Typically a council will charge people receiving attendance allowance (AA) the equivalent of 50% of this allowance each week towards the cost of their home care. Where home care is of a limited nature, the full cost may be charged if this is less than 50% of AA. In one London borough, for example, 601 people out of a possible 840 were paying 50% of their AA, amounting to £664,000 in the current year.

> '*Because AA is paid to help individuals provide for their home care, a higher cost could be paid by clients. Every 5% increase would generate an extra £145,000. But....the percentage charge cannot be set so high that it acts as a disadvantage for people to claim.*'
> Comment to a charging survey carried out among members of NCCA, 1997

The disability living allowance (DLA) was also further threatened. In an authority in the North East, it was proposed that those receiving the middle rate of DLA should raise their contribution to the costs of their day care from £4 a week to £4 a day. For those receiving the higher rate of DLA, contributions of £9 a day might be expected. As a result, a number of those attending day centres ceased going.

In a nearby authority those receiving the higher rate DLA saw their total average charge rise from £9 to £21.50 for five days a week day centre attendance. This increase was introduced without any consultation and there was consideration of extending it to those receiving the middle rate as well. This authority, when challenged, said that there were no authoritative guidelines by which it should abide.

There was particular concern that this policy was reducing the number of those with mental health problems attending day centres in this authority as they were not affected by increased charges if only attending one day a week.

The introduction of new types of charging

Local authorities demonstrated their powers of invention in adding to the list of charges that can be incurred. One move was to charge for aids and adaptations. A county council introduced four categories of charges for these, ranging through no charge for those on income support, £10 for those receiving AA, the full cost for those with more than £16,000 of savings and the cost up to £40 for those with less than £16,000 but not in receipt of benefits.

In other contexts charges were extended to people who were previously exempt from them. One county introduced charges in the change over from a formerly uncharged indirect payment scheme to a direct payment scheme. A postal survey of users of the scheme suggested that 19 people would have to give up work as a result. Local reaction was furious.

> *'What is society telling young disabled people? Don't get an education or any qualifications because you will never benefit from your endeavours. If you need a personal assistant, you will be taxed in such a way as to be kept at income support level. This is not the way to go forward.'*
> Comment to a charging survey carried out among members of NCCA, 1997

As Frances Hasler of the Centre for Independent Living observed in response to the NCCA Changing Survey, most assumptions about charging are based on an assumption that most disabled people do not work.

Failure to provide services

Another way in which local authorities defray the costs of services is simply by not providing them. Examples were forthcoming of authorities:

- encouraging individuals into residential care because the cost of home care would be higher (the perverse incentive);

- delaying the assessment process until the following financial year;

- restricting assessments only to those who are judged to have 'high need';

- refusing to help householders to sell their house to meet care costs.

Such deliberately obstructive procedures run completely against the principles of good community care.

There is, therefore, ample evidence, that the anxieties that prompted research into charging policies and practices in the first place have not been allayed and that many people, as a result of local charging policies, may not be receiving the help and support that good community care requires. Very recently, a Mencap (1999) survey has confirmed that nearly all social services departments charge people with learning disabilities for day centre attendance and other services and about half charge people whose only income is income support. Some people had stopped using services altogether because they could not afford to pay.

Recent research from Southwark

One recent piece of research evidence on the impact of means tested charges has come from a survey of four London authorities (Southwark Comunity Care Forum, 1998). This reported that in Southwark 3% of users had withdrawn from one or more services 'because they could not afford it' and, overall, 10% had stopped receiving some services because of worries over charges. Most felt they lacked adequate information on charging policies and found appeal processes difficult to follow. The study concluded that the level of charges was at the limit of what was acceptable without risking further significant fall off in service uptake.

Statutory versus voluntary sector

Members of voluntary organisations have expressed particular worries over the ways in which local authority policies impinge on them. For example, a decision has been taken in at least one London borough to start charging for services provided by the voluntary sector. This can raise difficulties with a voluntary organisation's charter as well as create confusion among users, some of whom may not be paid for by the local authority and so not liable for charges.

A further issue still being debated is exactly how far a charity should help to provide services that the state should properly provide.

Conclusion

The White Paper *Modernising Social Services* made welcome statements about the inequity of different levels of charges around the country and criticised the poor quality of information on charging made available to service users. It spelt out the case for fair access to services which accords with national standards. The majority Report of the Royal Commission on Long Term Care has suggested a division between personal care, living and accommodation costs, with personal care remaining free even in residential settings. It has not, however, recommended the abolition of means tested local authority charges for 'hotel' and living expenses for older people. This is disappointing in view of the evidence of the effects of such charges as summarised in this discussion. While awaiting the Audit Commission's report on charges and the Long Term Care Charter, it seems unlikely that the Government will decide against charging for essential social care and this means we should expect means testing for services to continue. We need further research to establish beyond reasonable doubt that the benefits of charging to local authorities' budgets are offset by both their administrative costs and the hidden costs to individuals and their families.

This section draws on the following sources:

Baldwin, S. and Lunt, N. (1996) *Charging Ahead: The development of local authority charging policies for community care,* Bristol: Policy Press.

Balloch, S. and Robertson, G. (1994) *Charging for Social Care,* London: NISW.

Becker, S. (1997) *Responding to Poverty: The politics of cash and care,* Harlow: Longman.

Bennett, F. (1996) *Highly Charged: Policy issues surrounding charging for non-residential care*, York: Joseph Rowntree Foundation.

Chetwynd, M. and Ritchie, J. in collaboration with Reith, L. and Howard, M. (1996) *The Cost of Care: The impact of charging policy on the lives of disabled people,* Bristol: Policy Press.

Clark, H., Dyer, S. and Horwood, J. 1998) *That Bit of Help,* Bristol: Policy Press.

Kestenbaum, A. (1997) *Disability: Related costs and charges for community care,* London: Disablement Income Group.

Local Government Management Board (1997) *Community Care Trends 1997 Report,* London: LGMB.

Mencap (1999) *Fully Charged: How local authority charging is harming people with a learning disability,* London: Mencap Campaigns Department.

National Consumer Council (1995) *Charging Consumers for Social Services: Local authority policy and practice,* London: NCC.

Royal Commission on Long Term Care (1999) *With Respect to Old Age: Long Term Care – Rights and Responsibilities*, Cm.4192, London: The Stationery Office.

Secretary of State (1998) *Modernising Social Services: Promoting independence; improving protection; raising standards,* Cm.4169, London: The Stationery Office.

Southwark Community Care Forum (1998) *Charging for Care: A study of the impact of means tested charging for community care services*, London: SCCF.

Chapter 10

Housing and Community Care

Ian Bradford and Sue Balloch

Housing is a vital component of community care and it is often the key to independent living. The Griffiths Report (DoH, 1988) played down the role of housing in community care and angered housing agencies by referring to this as restricted to 'bricks and mortar' with no social or interagency significance. However, the White Paper which followed recognised that the community care reforms should aim to enable people to remain at home, or in a homely setting in the community, if that is what they want.

It advised that housing's responsibilities should include:

- care and repair and staying put schemes to provide advice and help to elderly owner occupiers;

- adaptations to enable people with disabilities to stay in their own homes;

- specialised accommodation as an option;

- services collaboration with housing authorities, housing associations and other providers in developing plans for housing in community care;

- housing needs assessment as part of the assessment of care needs.

The Department of Health has since gone considerably further, stating that:

> 'In developing joint strategies housing, health and social services authorities should work together to review the range of provision available and examine the use of equipment and adaptations, support schemes including floating support, domiciliary care services, the role of residential care, and the use of and requirements for general and specialised housing.'

In spite of this, there is considerable evidence that authorities are failing to meet the housing needs of vulnerable people. The Audit Commission's report *Home Alone* identified a range of problems, including:

- people placed in unsuitable housing not receiving the practical help they need to cope with everyday living;

- vulnerable tenants abandoning their tenancies because of avoidable problems such as rent arrears;

- long waits for routine home improvements such as stair lifts;

- difficult to let sheltered housing or shortfalls in supported housing;

- inadequate information about people's needs and the available housing stock;

- the poor quality of much social housing.

To this we should add:

- the lack of choice experienced by those compelled to enter residential care because of the lack of community services and/or local authorities unwilling to provide necessary domiciliary care for low or no charge;

- problems experienced by people with community care needs who may be homeless or living in some form of temporary accommodation, such as direct access hostels, and who might prefer to live in ordinary housing and use mainstream services.

Work carried out for Care & Repair England and the Anchor Trust represents the beginnings of a methodology to demonstrate the cost effectiveness of addressing poor housing needs compared to other options such as residential care. This is at an early stage but is expected to add weight to the accepted view that care at home is not only best for the individual concerned but also usually offers greater value for money. While there are many examples of good practice, Care & Repair England has found that some working arrangements serve to thwart the effective collaboration between agencies that is necessary if people are to be able to stay in their own homes. For example, some social services authorities implement assessment criteria which effectively hinder clients in their efforts to secure mandatory disabled facilities grants. More and more demands are also being made on people to pay for their own home repairs, adaptations or equipment.

On a positive note, as explained in *Shaping Futures*, a paper being prepared for the Joseph Rowntree Foundation, 'new developments are beginning to change the traditional community care agenda'. The growth of supported housing, or accommodation with access to support services, is challenging traditional conceptions of residential homes.

The most recent figures from Laing and Buisson show a decline in numbers entering residential care. The view in some quarters is that the traditional residential home will feature much less in the next century. Other developments include grouped housing and villages for older people and the development of a range of patterns of home support appropriate for rural areas. There are significant components of social and health care skills and expertise in the day to day work of supported housing which are either being acquired through staff development or contracted in. Independent living, autonomy through support, increasing the period of health in old age, decreasing the numbers of people using acute beds and the amount of time spent in them are combining to promote rehabilitation once again, including in care homes. Rehabilitation in this new sense is interdisciplinary and aimed at increasing social and not just physical functioning. The outcomes are defined in terms of what people want to achieve.

Housing 21 endorses the idea of reinvented sheltered housing as a practical reality. In the London Borough of Redbridge, for example, 'the local authority is working with three housing associations to transfer and reshape its entire stock of sheltered housing and residential care homes' (Phillips and Fletcher, 1999 p.25). Housing 21 has taken over five schemes comprising more than 250 older people's homes.

Here we need to distinguish between supported housing, which is a generic term for any form of housing with help on hand, and sheltered housing, which is mainly provided for older people with a resident warden. Very sheltered housing could blur the distinction between living at home and living in institutions, and therefore prevent independence in sheltered housing being treated in the same way as if older people were in their own home. It is important that a move to sheltered housing should be a move to a new home in which the tenant remains independent, rather than a move towards dependent living in nursing or residential care.

Supporting people

Funding of such projects can be a major problem. The Government's Consultation Document *Supporting People* has proposed measures to help vulnerable people remain independent in the community, including rough sleepers, drug users and ex-offenders. It is based on an inter-departmental review which focused on housing benefit payments for support and counselling perceived by the Department of Social Security (DSS) as excessive. *Supporting People* proposes bringing together housing benefit paid for support services, the supported housing management grant and other existing funding into a specific grant to be distributed to local authorities for them to apply at the local level according to need. It also suggests creating incentives for local housing, social services and probation services to work together with a cross-authority fund to deal with the particular needs of people who do not naturally fit into any individual local authority area.

The specific grant has potential to bring funding for support closer to the point of delivery and closer to parallel provision such as social services funding. It could allow for the transfer of funds as residential services are reshaped and direct payments to individuals increased. The allocation and monitoring of the specific grant could also provide a boost to the development of local authority strategies on housing and support, representing a significant increase in accountability of provider to purchaser.

However, in their submissions to the Government, both the Local Government Association (LGA) and the National Housing Federation (NHF) criticised a lack of detail in the proposals, which could lead to what the NHF call 'fundamental gaps in equities and uncertainties.' In effect the specific grant will take benefit away from individuals and replace it with project funding, although the LGA and NHF both point to the lack of any detailed argument for this. As the LGA put it, 'there is an overwhelming case for there to be a continuing role for housing benefit in meeting a degree of counselling and support costs', on grounds of both principle and pragmatism. The removal of the statutory rights of the individual, represented by housing benefit, could also be construed as contrary to the *Modernising Social Services* ethos of promoting independent living and direct payments.

There is also the danger of missing an opportunity to create a fully coherent funding system that takes account of parallel residential and community care funding. The DSS has held on to payments for care and support services to those with 'preserved rights' living in residential homes and has thus created a powerful disincentive to providing alternative care packages for those involved. This is another anomaly that needs to be addressed.

Supported housing relies on funding from other sources in addition to housing benefit: some providers of supported housing place intensive housing management costs within mainstream rents; some tenants pay all of their disability living allowance or attendance allowance towards the cost of their services; health authorities provide funds for housing for people who have left long stay hospitals. All these and more need to be reconciled within the single budget so that supported housing can be properly and fairly financed. It is to be hoped that payments to individuals from this budget will not be means tested, establishing the principle that people should not have to pay for essential support services.

This section draws on the following sources:

Arnold, P., Bochel, H., Brodhurst, S. and Page, D. (1993) *Community Care: The housing dimension,* York: Joseph Rowntree Foundation.

Audit Commission (1998) *Home Alone: The role of housing in community care,* London: Audit Commission.

Care & Repair England (1998) *Submission to the Royal Commission on Long Term Care* (unpublished).

Department of Health (1989) *Caring for People: Community care in the next decade and beyond,* Cm.849, London: HMSO.

Department of Health and Department of the Environment (1997) *Housing and Community Care: Establishing a strategic framework,* London: Department of Health.

Department of Health (1998) *Community Care: An agenda for action* (The Griffiths Report), London: HMSO.

Griffiths, S. and Watson, L. (1999) *Revenue Funding and Tenant Choice in*

Supported Housing, Pathways Research and Griffiths Research for the Carr Gomm Society (unpublished).

Means, R. (1993) 'Housing and community care' in J. Johnson and R. Slater (eds.) *Ageing and Later Life,* London: Sage Publications, p.310-318.

Means, R. (1996) 'From 'special needs' housing to independent living?', *Housing Studies,* 11, 2, p.207-231.

Means, R. and Smith, R. (1996) *Community Care, Housing and Homelessness: Issues, obstacles and innovative practice,* Bristol: Policy Press.

Phillips, M. and Fletcher, P. (1999) 'Home but not alone', *Community Care,* 21 January, p.24-25.

Secretary of State (1998) *Modernising Social Services: Promoting independence; improving protection; raising standards,* Cm.4169, London: The Stationery Office.

Smart, G. and Means, R. (1997) *Housing and Community Care: Exploring the role of home improvement agencies,* Oxford: Anchor Trust and Care & Repair England.

Chapter 11

Community care and substance misuse service provision

Fiona Hackland

> '*There is no war on drugs. There is and always has been a war on drug users.*'
> John Mordaunt writing in *The Users' Voice*

Assessment and eligibility criteria

Assessment of drug users is often delegated by social services to local provider services which have expertise in the management of drug users. This can result in better assessment of drug problems but may also result in poor assessment of other related social problems. Standards for assessment of those with drug and alcohol problems have been defined by the Social Service Inspectorate but have been poorly implemented at a practice level.

SCODA's research (1996) has suggested that delays in assessment or accessing funding have been significant for this client group. Drug misusers require speedy access to assessment and subsequent residential care for a number of reasons, including:

* the increased health risks of continued drug use;

* the increased risk to children of drug users;

* missing windows of opportunity when drug users are actively seeking help;

* the damage that continued crime can cause to the community.

This lack of speed in carrying out assessments has a disproportionately detrimental effect on those groups most marginalised within the drug using population, for example offenders, parents.

Evidence suggests that eligibility criteria are narrowing to accept only those in most urgent need. This narrowing of criteria begs the question of what will be accepted as urgent need and who defines what urgent need is. This focus upon urgent need inhibits any preventative role for community care provision.

Access to services

Drug misusers' access to treatment has been impeded by factors such as assessment procedures, eligibility criteria and financial management strategies which fail to take account of the chronic, relapsing nature of drug misuse. Drug misusers often require repeat episodes of treatment. However, access to community care funding has been reduced by factors such as the imposition of time limits upon placements, and upon the time frames within which repeat assessment and funding episodes will be considered.

Establishment of these strategies may in part be due to a value base which views drug misuse as evidence of weakness and as a self inflicted condition. When seeking funding for treatment drug misusers must be seen to be committed to being drug free. Relapse is viewed as a lack of commitment, rather than an aspect of drug misuse which reflects more upon the nature of the condition, than upon the commitment of the individual drug misuser.

Lack of access has also had a differential impact upon vulnerable groups such as people with children and prisoners due for release. This is mainly due to disputes about funding responsibilities and budgets: for example, lack of agreement to fund children by care managers because of the extra burden upon community care budgets, accompanied by reluctance of social service departments responsible for children to fund children from child care budgets.

> *'For those who have managed to access drug treatment, many are expected to tail off their methadone prescriptions at a rate which tests the limits of human endurance...'*
> A doctor writing in *The Users' Voice*

Access for people with children can also be impeded even before assessment, due to fears the drug misusers may have about the institution of child care proceedings by social services. Seeking help is seen as less important than the potential loss of children.

A particularly complex matrix of problems affected prisoners due for release, including:

- as prisoners are seldom in prisons based in the local authority area they will be released to, purchasers enter into disputes about who has responsibility for assessment and funding, that is, the authority local to the prison, or local to the prisoner's residence upon release;

- the catch 22 situation where social services will not make decisions about funding and treatment until courts have approved treatment; courts would not approve treatment until social services had guaranteed funding.

Care management

A SCODA survey found that many community care allocations for drug services were overspent before the end of the financial year (in some cases half way through the year). Given that community care assessments are generally found to be resource-led rather than needs-led, this lack of resources will result in a restriction of service user access to any care.

Evidence from other organisations within drug and alcohol service provision suggests that up to 40% of community care budgets are spent on management, including assessment teams. It is questionable that this can be justified, particularly as outcomes of community care funding for drug misusers are seldom monitored.

Evidence also suggests that presentations by drug users for community care funding has risen by 14%. However, this has not been matched by funding in this area, which has only risen by 5%. Need is clearly not being met.

Service user choice

The reduction in numbers of residential rehabilitation beds has, in turn, restricted service user choice. Individual residential rehabilitation units base their treatment programmes upon different models of addiction and subsequent treatment responses to it. Before the implementation of community care, drug misusers could make decisions about residential placements based upon:

- the philosophy of treatment;

- treatment length;

- other factors, such as gender mix, location.

The lack of participation in service planning by ex or current drug misusuers has also contributed to narrowing of service user choice. Planning is dependent upon assessment of adequate service provision made by service purchasers rather than by those who use services.

> '*Whether we have choice of treatment options or not, if someone desires an addiction-free life, they will probably have to not use any drugs for a good while.*'
> Chronic relapser speaking out in *The Users' Voice*

Impact on service providers

In SCODA's experience the residential sector is the most fragile within drug services. This is predominantly due to community care impacting upon service provision in a number of ways:

- Residential services have national catchment areas. This results in service providers having to deal with a multiplicity of purchasers. Mechanisms are required at regional or national level for facilitating the provision of community care funding in a more coordinated way to service providers.

- Community care funding has often been restricted to limited time periods for residential stays, for example three to six months. Many residential services have had to drastically alter programmes which pre-existed community care.

Residential providers appear to have a wider funding base than community drug services – with many funding streams causing difficulty, especially community care. Cumulative effects on providers include increases in waiting lists, decrease in quality, less staff job security, reduction of 'core' services and greater risk of total or partial closure.

The perception of residential care being an expensive option has resulted in a rise in community-based treatment options such as structured day programmes. While these initiatives are clearly valuable and have a place in the treatment of drug users, they are not necessarily a cheaper option to residential care.

> *'Eventually I managed to get me a hospital bed to detox in. It was actually part of a rehabilitation programme and what we did there was amazing. Somehow all my fears of institutions were destroyed.'*
> Andy writing in *The Users' Voice*

The future

Evidence gathered by SCODA throughout the period of community care implementation suggests a pattern of narrowing of service provision and service user choice. The following recommendations were made in SCODA's report on its survey on the impact of community care:

- Social services departments should review urgently their community care procedures for drug misusers.

- Social services departments should review their eligibility criteria, in order to ensure that drug misusers leaving prison are assessed prior to their discharge.

- In the light of the Department of Health task force's conclusion about the chronic relapsing nature of drug misuse, social services departments should review their eligibility criteria so that no restriction is placed on eligibility by any previous period of support within any time period.

- Social services departments should set and publish the maximum time period within which a community care assessment will be undertaken: these should be monitored and reported on annually.

- Both assessors and care managers should be trained and competent in issues concerning drug misuse.

- Social services departments should identify clearly specific budgets for drug (and alcohol) support under community care arrangements.

Our subsequent exploration of the impact of community care upon drug misusers and service providers suggests that these recommendations remain pertinent.

> *'In the absence of drug-free treatment beds we need to be contained by maintenance doses (legal ones preferably) of our drug(s) of addiction and encouraged/mentored back into education, training and employment.'*
> Andrea Efthimiou-Mordaunt, Editor, writing in *The Users' Voice*

This section draws on the following sources:

Department of Health (1988) *Community Care: An agenda for action* (The Griffiths Report), London: HMSO.

Standing Committee on Drug Abuse (SCODA) (1996) *The Eye of a Needle*, London: SCODA.

Social Services Inspectorate (1994) *Commissioning Community Care: Substance misuse*, London: SSI.

Issues of *The Users' Voice: A forum for ex/current addict drug users*, London: John Mordaunt Trust.

Chapter 12

Social services departments and their staff

Enid Levin

Introduction

This discussion concentrates on the impact of the NHS and Community Care Act 1990 from the perspective of social services. It differentiates between the Act on the one hand and the responses to it and the resources for it on the other. It takes account of the wider environment into which the Act was introduced and more recent changes signalled by the new Government agenda, with its major policy thrust towards much closer working between health and social services and other sectors. The discussion is based mainly on the results of a Department of Health funded study of social work and community care post implementation in local authority social service departments (Levin and Webb, 1997), and also on research in progress to compare different models of front line collaboration between health and social care and their outcomes for service users and carers. A final section, based on the NISW Workforce Studies (Balloch, McLean and Fisher, 1999), addresses the wider issues in ensuring a human resources policy to implement the aims of community care.

Effects on the structures of social services departments

The implementation of the Children Act 1989 together with the NHS and Community Care Act 1990 has resulted in the biggest change in the organisation and delivery of social care since unified social services departments were created almost thirty years ago. This legislation accelerated the already existing trend towards re-specialisation in work with different service user groups, spurred on in the 1980s by child protection issues and the requirement for approved social workers in mental health. Social services departments are now organised into two broad divisions and work with children and families is undertaken separately from community care, which covers work with adults. This split is both vertical and horizontal, running throughout almost all the organisation below directorate level so that each arm of the operation has its own assistant directors, service plans, front line teams and lines of accountability.

This structural change was not prescribed and might be viewed as a major but unintended consequence of the two Acts. It is one source of the many new interfaces within social services and with other agencies which now have to be bridged and managed because families with problems straddle client groups, as does general practice, other health services and agencies.

The senior managers and practitioners in 52 community care teams and three SSDS in our study were generally positive about this development for the reasons that work with adults had achieved a higher profile than before and attracted qualified social workers with an interest in the specialism, that teams were more cohesive and that adults benefited from being served by separate teams from children. The 'downsides of specialism' were also identified, including the resultant new interfaces. There were concerns, too, about the impact of specialisation on the future of social work as one profession and its implications for training.

Within community care services there is less uniformity in the arrangements and less agreement about the degree of specialisation in the various client groups, with the exception of discrete community mental health teams. Some departments have integrated teams for older people, adults with physical and with learning disabilities and others separate by age group or disability. Reorganisation, often resource-led, continues in this branch of the operation and the advantages and disadvantages of the various arrangements for service users have not been widely researched or debated. Further reconfigurations have taken place or are planned to facilitate closer working with health: for example, by locating teams in health centres or aligning named social workers with community nurses and general practitioners.

Effects on the roles and tasks of social workers

The philosophy of the 1990 Act with its emphasis on promoting independence and enabling people to live at home has widespread support among social work managers and practitioners. The main concern expressed is that resources available for the purpose put limits on the degree to which the Act can be fully implemented and achieve its promise in the context of rising demands and expectations.

The right to an assessment of individual need and the duty to assess need was the part of the Act itself which the 300 front line practitioners in our survey most often identified as having the biggest impact on their jobs. Assessment became a service and the volume of such work increased with the transfer of the care element of income support from social security for those entering residential and nursing home care, and new arrangements for those previously referred and assessed directly by home care organisers. The responses of departments to the key objectives in the White Paper of targeting those in greatest need, moving to an enabling role, and making increasing use of the independent sector, as well as to the key tasks and processes of care management in the guidance and to the changes in health, also affected the emphasis and content of the social worker's workload, as eligibility criteria were developed, in-house arrangements were made to separate the commissioning and providing functions and to contract with the independent sector, and new systems and procedures for care management were set up.

By 1996, care management had become the core business of community care teams and continues to be so. On our evidence, the great majority of practitioners are engaged in assessing, devising care plans, setting up care packages and monitoring and reviewing them. Most cost and purchase care packages are subject to the approval of team managers but budgets are devolved to team rather than individual care manager level. Care management was described as making the work 'more managed' and 'more manageable', leading to greater consistency, clarity and accountability; but also as shifting the balance of work to concentrate on higher levels of disability, more crisis work and more emphasis on arranging practical help, which has always been part of the task. The changes were described as both 'liberating' and 'restricting', leading to less professional autonomy and more defensive practice but also to greater flexibility and choice, within limits. Social work skills are highly relevant, have been adapted and are used in care management. Roles and tasks which have moved down the agenda are preventative and rehabilitative work, group work, outreach and development, spending time with individuals to enable them to make life decisions at their own pace, counselling and the provision of long term emotional support.

Commissioning services from a range of providers in the mixed economy of care was one of the activities which had a substantial effect on the everyday work of practitioners. There was a consensus that the difference that the policy changes had made to their work was that they spent 'more time at the desk and less time with service users', and that this development was driven by the volume of administrative tasks and paperwork required at each stage of the care management process. One fifth of the social workers' and 27% of the social work assistants' time on their last day at work had been spent in face to face contact with service users, a proportion which is lower than that reported before the changes. For every hour spent in face to face contact with service users, a further four hours were required to set up the care package. In broad terms, the findings from the NISW Workforce Studies support this picture of staff feeling that they are spending more time on administration.

The increase in the volume of paperwork and administrative tasks associated with each stage of the care management process is again an arguably unintended consequence of the policy changes and the new local systems and procedures put in place to implement it. This 'bureaucratisation of social work' is consistently reported in the first wave of monitoring and inspection reports and community care studies following the 1990 Act, and some departments have been reviewing their arrangements with a view to streamlining the process and assessing the scope for redressing the balance through better routine administrative and clerical support.

The scope, content and emphasis of the work of social services departments and the front line practitioners within them has shifted substantially since the changes, despite many continuities, and care management has become the core business of community care teams. Tensions remain between the more systematic, consistent approach to access and assessment and the provision of more flexible individualised care packages. Some service user groups and individuals, in the opinion of practitioners, may have benefited more than others, both in terms of the intensity of care package and its responsiveness. Constraints on budgets limit the extent to which the concept of community care achieves its promise.

The workforce

The study *Social Work and Community Care* (Levin and Webb, 1997) focused primarily on social workers, while this next section addresses the social services workforce as a whole. The White Paper *Modernising Social Services* acknowledges that 'people who work in social care are called on to respond to some of the most demanding, often distressing and intractable human problems' (p.84). Studies carried out in England, Scotland and Northern Ireland between 1992 and 1998 by NISW, and brought together in *Social Services: Working Under Pressure* (Balloch, McLean and Fisher, 1999), show that those working in the statutory social services still possess the commitment and dedication on which a sensitive and skilled response to such problems ultimately depends. Job satisfaction in the workforce is high, particularly among home care staff, and grows when staff are able to provide people with the resources and support they need.

There are two key factors impinging on the implementation of community care. First, the research confirms that the social services workforce is carrying out its responsibilities under considerable pressure – pressure which is undermining that competence and confidence that the White Paper describes as 'an essential component of the modernisation of social services' (p.85). Stress appears to affect managers most — the very people with the key responsibility to effect changes. A substantial proportion of staff report abuse from service users and their relatives, and for a sizeable minority of black staff this includes racism from both service users and colleagues. Staff also report spending more time on paperwork, which undermines their attempts to do the job as they think it should be done.

Secondly, the research points to the difficulties, despite substantial investment, of delivering sufficient training to underpin the changing focus of management and practice. At the time of the study, three quarters of the workforce — mainly women working in residential and home care – had no educational or professional qualifications, and limited access to training. Amongst these groups, less than 10% were involved in gaining an NVQ. Most social work staff were qualified but three quarters did so before the

NHS and Community Care Act 1990, and may possess practice philosophies from an earlier era in which the service user's voice was less prominent. At the second interview in 1995/96, 40% of staff reported being unable to secure training they sought.

Overall, the research suggests that the workforce may not be reskilling fast enough to match the emerging agendas. In particular, staff whose qualifications were acquired before the community care legislation, and before the views of service users became more widely acknowledged, may find the current climate distinctly challenging. Central Government cannot expect to achieve empowering services for users through the community care changes and Best Value in the new regime for inspection, regulation, training and service delivery set out in *Modernising Social Services*, unless it also invests in staff. One important way this could be achieved is by extending the involvement of service users in the education and training of the workforce, including in the key policy making bodies, the national training organisations.

This section draws on the following sources:

Balloch, S., McLean, J. and Fisher, M. (eds.) (1999) *Social Services: Working under pressure,* Bristol: Policy Press.

Levin, E. and Webb, S. (1997) *Social Work and Community Care: Changing roles and tasks,* confidential report to the Department of Health (unpublished).

Secretary of State (1998) *Modernising Social Services: Promoting independence; improving protection; raising standards,* Cm.4169, London: The Stationery Office.

Chapter 13

Conclusions

This review and the consultation exercises that accompanied it have attempted to review critically the implementation of the NHS and Community Care Act 1990. The authors have drawn on a variety of sources of evidence to provide a comprehensive assessment of the effects of the Act's implementation. They have tried to explore and reflect both the diversity of views and the diversity of stakeholders. In these conclusions we draw out some of the themes emerging from the review and, where possible, highlight actions which these conclusions suggest.

Needs-based community care

As a piece of legislation the NHS and Community Care Act was designed to meet central Government's objective of a cash-limited and needs-based approach to community care. It can be regarded as generally successful in terms of the cash limits but much more uncertain in terms of meeting needs. Means and Smith (1998) point out that 'local authorities are now responsible not only for operating a needs-based yet cash-limited system but also for the rationing consequences of trying to provide both elements' (p.230). There has also been a shifting of the boundaries of NHS continuing care to local authorities, as illustrated in the case brought by Pamela Coughlan against North and East Devon Health Authority (July 1999). In this case, the Appeal Court's refusal to back an earlier High Court ruling that nursing care should be provided by the NHS rather than social services has been greeted with delight by central Government because of the savings this will allow to the NHS. It has, however, been greeted with dismay by disabled people and voluntary organisations, deeply concerned that the cost of nursing care in nursing homes will still be means tested. Confusion over the difference between 'nursing care', free at the point of delivery, and 'social care', which is means tested, remains one of the most problematic issues for individuals needing long term health and personal care. We agree with the Royal Commission on Long Term Care that all those needing such care should receive it free of charge.

Funding

The continued underfunding of community care services has prevented them from being truly 'needs-led'. The Association of Directors of Social Services and the Local Government Association contend that, since 1992/93, the basic amounts of personal social services standard spending assessments have actually decreased by over 6% in real terms. Although the 1998 White Paper announced a £3 billion pound increase in spending on social services, most of this has been ring-fenced and will only contribute to the community care budget in specific instances. As a result, local authorities continue to introduce new charging policies for those receiving their services and private spending continues to grow, creating a situation which particularly penalises those on lower incomes. Our society at the end of the twentieth century is still divided by income differentials. As the New Policy Institute, funded by the Joseph Rowntree Foundation, has shown, there are major gaps between the spending powers of different social groups and their ability to meet the costs of care, particularly in old age.

Uncertainty over the balance between public and private funding for community care is reflected in the majority and minority reports of the Royal Commission on Long Term Care and in the Government's reluctance to act on the proposals. We believe that both needs and rights-based approaches to community care demand a level playing field for meeting the costs of health care, personal care and living, so that all individuals are able to participate fully in normal political and social life.

Rights and citizenship

Those contributing to this review believe that the Act and its subsequent implementation are open to further major criticism: namely, the inability and reluctance of the majority of agencies to replace professionally dominated services with ones based on users' rights and recognition of users' expertise in defining outcomes.

Because the NHS and Community Care Act was designed to curtail central Government spending and to give voice to a narrow, consumerist philosophy of social welfare, it has subsequently offered more obstacles than assistance to a new ethos of user empowerment and service integration. It certainly has not supported the rights-based approach to community care that was so prominent in the submissions to this review. The review illustrates a number of interconnected themes, the most important of which is the way in which the needs-based model of community care integral to the Act has little in common with a rights-based model linked directly to a revitalised concept of citizenship. As noted in the Introduction (Chapter 1), the rights-based model of citizenship underpins the growing user movements and is well illustrated by direct payments. Within community care it upholds the expectation of services which will support maximum independence for users with minimum intrusion into personal lives. We recognise the challenge that this poses to the traditional, needs-based delivery of services and to the working practices and training of staff who have been in charge of these. Some will undoubtedly see it as threatening.

Progress and obstacles

Several contributions to the review have noted that empowering service users to give them real choice requires new ways of working, including planning and implementation of partnerships. The review illustrates considerable progress: the growth of user controlled self advocacy organisations which have promoted independent living schemes, the implementation of direct payments and the introduction of user controlled services. Less institutional forms of service have been developed for people with mental health problems and learning difficulties, combining living in ordinary houses in the community with support schemes for further education, employment and leisure activities. For older people, both supported and sheltered housing have provided readily acceptable alternatives to residential care. An increase in black and minority ethnic staff has accompanied the development of both specialist services and changes in mainstream provision to meet the needs of members of black and minority ethnic communities.

Some developments, however, are running counter to such progress. As Mike Fisher notes, 'for people with mental health problems, the current direction is unmistakably towards greater coercion, not greater choice' (Chapter 2). For many older people, and particularly those with dementia, society's attitude to their rights lags far behind that towards other groups. For many black and minority ethnic groups services remain both inappropriate and underfunded. For drugs misusers access to treatment and rehabilitation is often impossible at a time when motivation is present. These national shortcomings illustrate the patchwork nature of developments in community care since 1993.

Users' expertise

This review shows that recognition of users' rights requires sustained and serious acknowledgement by policy makers and practitioners of users' expertise in understanding their own needs and defining the outcomes that they want from services. It is this expertise which properly underpins 'evidence based practice'. Most recent outcomes work reflects a health care model relating to functional ability or mental states rather than quality of life in the community. The review suggests that, if this model is applied more widely, it may intensify social exclusion by spotlighting disability rather than ability. As Turner (1999) suggests:

> 'A major development project by disabled people is needed to discover outcome measures in terms of the removal of physical and social barriers, rather than the values and goals of the service providers that inform most current outcome measures.'

The Shaping Our Lives project has already gone far in its promotion of user-defined outcomes and has recently received further funding from the Joseph Rowntree Foundation to continue this work. However, such progress will only have full impact in improving community care when the expertise of the people who use services becomes as highly valued as professional opinions. In view of the Government's development of the performance assessment framework for social services the definition and development of user-led outcomes now carries a special urgency.

Mapping inequalities

Several of the contributions highlight user involvement. Vivien Lindow, for example, notes that authors have concluded that progress being made towards user involvement in community care services is piecemeal or patchy. This has prompted a suggestion for a mapping exercise to inform Government of existing inequalities and disseminate good practice. The mapping should survey community care for both geographical inequalities and inequalities between different service user groupings, and include the existence of independent, democratic organisations of service users. Such an exercise should be led by the expertise of disabled people holding a range of perspectives. It should also seek to address under-representation of older community care service users in user movements and explore the perspectives of older people on their rights and needs. Service users from minority ethnic communities also have essential expertise to contribute to such a mapping exercise.

Acute and preventative services

The review emphasises serious inconsistencies in policy and practice. For example, providing intensive services for users with multiple needs has led to a reduction in those preventative services which enable service users to avoid dependency and may even have increased costs. Jo Moriarty points out in Chapter 6 that:

> 'One of the key issues for the future is how to distinguish better between community care services that are best delivered in an intensive way to a highly targeted group of people and those universalist services, such as a short term care attendant scheme for people discharged from hospital, whose cost effectiveness would have been reduced had it only been available to a restricted group.'

It is perverse and counter-productive that, in a drive to target limited resources on those in greatest need, we are undermining those lower level services that can enable people to retain their independence and prevent them from needing more intensive, and more costly, care.

Skills and knowledge of the workforce

Good outcomes in community care require more than just technical skills: they also require good processes, and this is why user groups place so much emphasis on empowerment as the key. One of the enduring impressions of the consultation underpinning this review is that working in community care requires new skills of people in whose education and training there has traditionally been a low level of investment – for example, older women working as care assistants in residential or domiciliary care.

Even those with qualifications in social care may not feel equipped to meet the challenge of empowering practice.

We have seen it argued in this review that the purchaser/provider split has led to an unnecessary barrier between service users and the most skilled staff, who often cease contact after assessment. One view among users is that if staff cannot make the transition to become empowering, they should not have a place in community care, and certainly direct payments will give some users the power to make these decisions. Another shortcoming is that the current level of user involvement in professional education and training is too little, too late, to make the changes required: users have little desire to undertake remedial work to undo what is perceived as the damage of traditional education and training.

Formal responsibility for reshaping the skills and knowledge of the social care workforce will lie with the new national training organisations. We envisage a UK inquiry into the skills and knowledge required to work in empowerment oriented, front line social care practice, underpinned by empirical work on current skills and knowledge use in order to build on and support the workforce. Increasingly, such a project will need to encompass health care as well as social care and housing professionals. The inquiry should be led by service users and might encompass both basic and post qualifying education and training for all sections of the workforce. It should include a curriculum design project to meet the education and training requirements identified by the inquiry, again led by users. Special attention should be given to the role of service users in professional education and training and to the position of service users who are also members of the workforce.

Care management

The theory of care management accords well with a rights-based approach to delivering community support. In practice, however, this review suggests that service users often find the availability of appropriate services is circumscribed by:

- financial restrictions experienced by local authorities;

- limitations that result from block contracts;

- failure to take user-defined outcomes into account.

In addition there is little evidence to suggest that care management has done much to foster the development of appropriate services for black and minority ethnic communities.

User-led organisations have been active in challenging these failings, and the development of direct payment schemes and the passing of legislation to allow this to happen has proved popular. Direct payments place care management under the control of users themselves, albeit with social services support. As Clare Evans (1998) has said:

'If the rhetoric of community care with its emphasis on individual packages of care through care management is to be a reality, the direct payments legislation should be welcomed by local authorities as an opportunity for them to enable service users to have more choice and control.'

As yet, however, there appears to be little evidence of such support from local authorities.

The increasing complexity of the market in social care provision has accompanied the development of care management. This was in part a product of the 1990 Act which sought to develop independent provision. However, this has proved a two-edged sword, extending the availability of independent provision but with no guarantee of quality services. With most residential services and over half of domiciliary services now provided by independent suppliers, implementation of the measures for quality control proposed in the *Modernising Social Services* White Paper are eagerly awaited. It will be important that a way is found for service users' views to be central to these.

Final remarks

Delivery of community care services using a rights-based approach could greatly enhance social inclusion. It requires a change in professional attitudes and behaviour to include the expertise of those who use services on an equal basis. Traditional social care attitudes of dependent clients looked after by experts who know best have no place in a society aiming to reduce social exclusion. Giving citizens the support they need to take part in the mainstream must involve reducing barriers to full participation by redefining rather than enhancing professional powers.

This section draws on the following sources:

Evans, C. (1998) 'User empowerment and direct payments' in Balloch, S. (ed.) *Outcomes of Social Care: A question of quality?* London: National Institute for Social Work

Howarth, C., Kenway, P., Palmer, G. and Street, C. (1998) 'Monitoring poverty and social exclusion, *JRF Findings*, D48.

Means, R. and Smith, R. (1998) *Community Care: Policy and practice,* second edition, Basingstoke: Macmillan.

Turner, M. (1999) Shaping Our Lives, Interim and Final Reports, London: NISW Policy Unit.